IDENTITY

FINDING PURPOSE THROUGH THE STORM

Cameron Kinley

Copyright © 2023 Cameron Kinley

All rights reserved.

ISBN-13: 979-8-218-22022-8

DEDICATION

This book is dedicated to my first football coach: Richard Kinley Sr. Thank you, Dad, for being my coach, but more importantly, for never forgetting to be my father first. You taught me how to approach this game the right way, leading me to become a champion on the field and in life.

ACKNOWLEDGEMENTS

There was only one teacher I took for all four years during my time at Lausanne: Dr. Nancy Graham. From Global Perspectives to Intro to Global Politics to two years of Anthropology, Dr. Graham always demanded the best out of me, never allowing me to settle for any less than my full potential. When I first decided to write this book, I immediately reached out to Dr. Graham for advice. Dr. Graham played a direct role in the editing process of this memoir, and I can't thank her enough for her willingness to be a part of this project.

I would also like to thank Chad Partee (@prodbydonee) for the cover design and Eric Echols (@soulifephotography) for the cover photography.

TABLE OF CONTENTS

INTRODUCTION 1
1 | THE QUESTION 3
2 | THE PROCESS.. 16
3 | THE SCRIPTURE 29
4 | THE STORM 41
5 | THE LEAP 53
6 | THE HARVEST 67
7 | THE DENIAL 80
8 | THE REVERSAL.. 90
9 | THE HARVEST PT. 2 99
10 | THE INTERVIEW 106
11 | THE REVELATION 114
GRATITUDE 121
ABOUT THE AUTHOR... 122

INTRODUCTION

In many ways, writing this book was a method of therapy. It has been over a year since I last played football. While I'm grateful for my career, I still find myself searching for answers to why everything had to end the way it did. My parents always taught me that football wasn't everything but just a part of who I was. However, when you've been doing something for more than 80% of your life, it becomes the majority of your identity.

My life revolved around the game of football. It cultivated my character, strengthened my faith, and taught me how to handle wins and losses in life. Without it, I found myself looking to fill an empty void. Though I had experienced some success off the field, I felt like my value decreased without being seen as a football player. I felt incomplete.

We all go through transitions in life. Whether it's a new job, relationship, or location...change happens. Amid change, a question that commonly pops up in our mind is, "What is God doing in my life?" In John 13:7, Jesus says, "You do not realize now what I am doing, but later you will understand." In these uncomfortable times of transition, we must trust in the preparation that God is taking us through.

I found myself in this position as I went from playing football in the NFL to beginning my career as an officer in the United States Navy. I had no issue with serving in the military. In fact, I looked forward to it. However, I felt like I never gained closure from my football career. I still feel like I had unfinished business. This left me wondering how the recent events in my life fit into God's plan.

While writing this book, I realized the answers were right in front of me the whole time. In fact, the answers appeared years ago. I just needed to take the time to go back and look for them. There is power in reflection. Reflection reminds us of our own growth. You might not be exactly where you want to be, but examining your past will help you realize that you are much further along than you used to be. In this growth, we begin to identify the true value of life.

Many other variables have contributed to my growth: my family, my relationship, my church, my mentors, my fraternity, my schools, etc. You will have to read my other books to hear about those areas. *Identity* will primarily focus on the journey I experienced through football. Whether you played sports or not, this journey will serve as an inspiration for your walk of life.

The stories you're about to read are full of truth and transparency. After reading *Identity*, you will be moved to reexamine the adversity and obstacles you've encountered. There's no need to delay. Take my hand and come along on this journey with me as we discover my identity. Here's my story. One that led to finding purpose through the storm.

1 | THE QUESTION

Richard Kinley Sr. grew up in Paris – not the romantic European capital you might be thinking of, though. I'm talking about Paris, Tennessee. A small country town with a population of just above 10,000 people.

He was raised in a 3-bedroom, 1-bathroom house with six other people: my grandmother, my grandfather, my two uncles, and my two aunties. Sharing one bedroom with his two older brothers, including a shared bed with my Uncle Vic, was all the motivation my father needed. He appreciated what his parents were able to provide, but he knew that he wanted to experience what was beyond his hometown.

And that's what he was able to do.

Dad's opportunity came from his ability to play football, which led him to receive a full-ride scholarship to play at the Division I level for Middle Tennessee State University. He played four seasons for the Blue Raiders as a defensive lineman and earned the starting job his junior and senior years. He graduated and hung up the cleats in 1991 and was soon involved with coaching youth football in the Nashville and Memphis areas.

My older brother, Jonathan (JB), was the first of the three boys to experience having my dad as a coach. I've only heard the horror stories about the 1-on-1 sessions that my dad would have with Jonathan in our backyard. As a kid, we used to think that our backyard was enormous, at least 50 yards in length. In reality, our backyard was half of that. Nonetheless, it was big enough for my dad to put JB to work. Jonathan went up and down that backyard more than a lawnmower ever would. Any time he dropped a pass from my dad, he had to run sprints. Not with a football, though. My dad would make JB catch baseballs with his bare hands. From a few close encounters with the ball, Jonathan developed some of the softest hands I've ever seen for a linebacker. Not only that, but those backyard sessions strengthened Jonathan's mindset. He became an undeniable football monster. Jonathan knew that if he could make it through those sessions with my dad, then he could make it through anything. He was rewarded for his perseverance.

Jonathan would go on to win Tennessee's Mr. Football award, given to the best high school defensive player in the state for each Division. He then played college ball at the University of Illinois, where he was a 3xAll-Big Ten linebacker and finished with 45.5 career tackles for loss, ranking him 3rd in school history. His success at the collegiate level allowed him to have an opportunity in the NFL for about three years with the Arizona Cardinals, Chicago Bears, and Dallas Cowboys.

As you can imagine, it was tough growing up in Jonathan's shadow. The pressure was real, and the years. He graduated and hung up the cleats in 1991 and was soon involved with coaching youth football in the Nashville and Memphis areas.

My older brother, Jonathan (JB), was the first of the three boys to experience having my dad as a coach. I've only heard the horror stories about the 1-on-1 sessions that my dad would have with Jonathan in our backyard. As a kid, we used to think that our backyard was enormous, at least 50 yards in length. In reality, our backyard was half of that. Nonetheless, it was big enough for my dad to put JB to work. Jonathan went up and down that backyard more than a lawnmower ever would. Any time he dropped a pass from my dad, he had to run sprints. Not with a football, though. My dad would make JB catch baseballs with his bare hands. From a few close encounters with the ball, Jonathan developed some of the softest hands I've ever seen for a linebacker. Not only that, but those backyard sessions strengthened Jonathan's mindset. He became an undeniable football monster. Jonathan knew that if he could make it through those sessions with my dad, then he could make it through anything. He was rewarded for his perseverance.

Jonathan would go on to win Tennessee's Mr. Football award, given to the best high school defensive player in the state for each Division. He then played college ball at the University of Illinois, where he was a 3xAll-Big Ten linebacker and finished with 45.5 career tackles for loss, ranking him 3rd in school history. His success at the collegiate level allowed him to have an opportunity in the NFL for about three years with the Arizona Cardinals, Chicago Bears, and Dallas Cowboys.

As you can imagine, it was tough growing up in Jonathan's shadow. The pressure was real, and the

1 | THE QUESTION

Richard Kinley Sr. grew up in Paris – not the romantic European capital you might be thinking of, though. I'm talking about Paris, Tennessee. A small country town with a population of just above 10,000 people.

He was raised in a 3-bedroom, 1-bathroom house with six other people: my grandmother, my grandfather, my two uncles, and my two aunties. Sharing one bedroom with his two older brothers, including a shared bed with my Uncle Vic, was all the motivation my father needed. He appreciated what his parents were able to provide, but he knew that he wanted to experience what was beyond his hometown.

And that's what he was able to do.

Dad's opportunity came from his ability to play football, which led him to receive a full-ride scholarship to play at the Division I level for Middle Tennessee State University. He played four seasons for the Blue Raiders as a defensive lineman and earned the starting job his junior and senior expectations were high. Jonathan set the standard for me and my younger brother, Richard. I wasn't nearly as athletically talented as Jonathan was, but that wasn't what it was about. It wasn't about me becoming like Jonathan, being the same caliber of athlete as him, or even becoming better than him. What mattered most was that I had the keys to becoming a legendary football player. Jonathan gave me the blueprint.

I watched Jonathan go through the college football recruiting process. Various Division I coaches came into our living room and pitched their best offer to him. I remember going on official visits with him and getting treated like royalty. I remember seeing how hard he would work in our garage during his high school off-seasons and whenever he would be home for the holidays from college. I remember our trips to the University of Illinois and seeing the banners of him on street poles and fans asking for his autograph as he dominated in the Big Ten. Most of all, though, I remember the humility Jonathan kept through all the recognition and the transparency he had with Richard and me about the challenges the game of football brought. He wanted to make sure that he set an example for us and helped us in any way he could to get us to the next level.

So, while following in his footsteps was daunting, it was also a blessing. Through my brother, I saw the possibility of dreams coming true. I saw the fruition of years and years of dedication to the game. I saw that I could go get it if I truly wanted it. I took every lesson I learned while being known as "JB's little brother," and I used it to pave my own route.

Identity

♦ ♦ ♦

My football journey began with the Memphis Falcons, my dad's youth organization that he started in 2004. My dad knew that it was always good to start them early; I was just five years old when I strapped the pads up for the first time. At age 5, I didn't realize that my dad was introducing me to a sport that would become more than just a game. It would become a teacher in my life. And it didn't take long for me to learn lessons. In fact, it started on that first day when I laced the cleats up.

My dad wanted to know who the fastest guy on the team was. He marked off 25 yards with two small, orange cones and lined all of us up at the first one. I knew the race was mine. Nobody in the neighborhood could keep up with me. In my mind, these kids were no different. I had this in the bag.

At the whistle, I lowered my head and blasted from the starting position with a smile. That smile quickly turned into a troubled look as I could see one of my teammates passing me out of my peripheral vision. I, in fact, did not have the race in the bag. I needed more than my overconfidence to win. It was my first loss in the game of football.

My confidence took a major hit. If it was one thing about young Cam, he hated to lose. Shoot, I still hate to lose. I was always a competitive kid. I wanted to be the best at everything I did. Winning was my validation. While in the car on the way home from practice, I told my dad that I wasn't good enough to play football and wasn't going back out there. I quit.

After dinner that night, my dad told me to stick around.

We sat at the kitchen table, and I got the first of many "Father-Coach to Son-Player" lectures. While I can't recall most of the words from that conversation, I remember my dad asking one question that has stuck with me forever: "Who are you going to be?"

"Who are you going to be?" would be the question that rang in my head as I continued the rest of my football career. Whenever I've encountered adversity throughout my career, I've asked myself, "Who are you going to be?". Anyone can be optimistic when everything goes their way, but when your back is up against the wall, "Who are you going to be?"

In his book *Strength to Love*, Dr. Martin Luther King Jr. says it best,

> "The ultimate measure of a man is not where he stands in moments of convenience and comfort, but where he stands at times of challenge and controversy."

In these times of challenge and controversy, nothing matters more than what you have on the inside of you. It doesn't matter how much money you have in your bank account, what kind of car you drive, what size house you live in...none of that. None of that will save you. When you strip away all the materialistic aspects, all you have left is who you truly are. Your identity. Your character. What you stand for. I ultimately believe that this is revealed in the most uncomfortable times, and the strength of your character will allow you to prevail.

And these hard times don't discriminate, even for a kid playing a sport for the first time. I wasn't exempt from facing adversity just because I was young. I also wasn't exempt from choosing how to respond to that adversity.

At the age of 5, my dad was able to get this message across to me, and I got right back on the field the next day. Who knows where I would be today if my dad had just let me walk away.

In many ways, I look at little league football as the glory days. I was having fun, playing the sport that I loved. Most of my time was spent playing offense, where I experienced the thrills of scoring touchdowns and leading my team to undefeated seasons and multiple championships. My favorite part, however, was the time I spent with Coach Kinley.

Growing up, my dad worked the graveyard shift in the logistics and operations management sector. While we were at school, he'd be home asleep. When we got home from school, he'd wake up and take us to football practice. After practice, he'd get cleaned up and head to work. Because of this grueling schedule, football practice was the only time I spent with my dad during the fall weekdays. Football was the backbone of our relationship.

It was tough seeing' my dad work that graveyard shift. I could see the exhaustion and weariness in his eyes. He never allowed this to be an excuse to complain, though. Neither of my parents complained. Even my mom when she decided to work full-time to support the family. My parents sacrificed a lot to put me and my siblings in the best situation possible. They both wanted to give us access to opportunities they didn't have in their childhood. I feel like that's why they put us in the private school system.

My sister, Nia, was the first to make the transition. My parents placed her at one of the top all-girls schools in the city. Richard and I went to the neighborhood elementary, and after picking us up from school, my mom would drive us to get Nia. The campus was like a college; we had to go through a gate to get in and pass lakes, swimming pools, and storied buildings. As I looked out the window, I thought I was in Disney World or somewhere. My sister flourished, and after a year, my mother decided that Richard and I should go to an all-boys private school. I was in the second grade.

I was excited to be attending a school like my sister's. In this new setting, I developed a solid academic foundation, grew in my faith, and built friendships I still hold today. However, the state-of-the-art buildings, quality food, and abundant resources couldn't cover a cold reality. Out of a class of around 80 boys, I was 1 of only 5 Black boys. Most days were awkward, at best, when I looked around and saw I was the only brown person in the room. The lunch was delicious, but I couldn't stand feeling like that all day in the classroom. I struggled to fit in. I told my mom I wanted to transfer schools, but she refused my request. My mom would not allow skin color to be a barrier and knew that I had to learn to be comfortable in an uncomfortable situation. She was my mom, so I did what I was told but still felt disadvantaged.

Most of my classmates came from very wealthy families. Their parents were doctors, lawyers, businessmen, and so forth. When I went on overnights, I was overwhelmed by the size of the houses and little luxuries that went unnoticed – like having one's own bedroom. There were televisions everywhere, pantries full of snacks, basketball hoops with glass backboards, swimming pools, ATVs...I could go on and on. It was like a movie set. Though I was mesmerized by the glamor, it also highlighted the differences in our lives. Everything in my life seemed like a struggle compared to theirs. Different music, different clothes, different family trips...Everything just felt

Identity

different. I started to question my own identity. I began to change how I talked and carried myself so that I might find acceptance in this new environment.

I was still playing football with the Memphis Falcons, and we practiced and played in a different part of town. At practice, my friends would say that I 'talked white' or 'acted white.' I started to feel like I didn't fit in with them either. I was living two lives, one at school with my white friends and one on the field with my Black friends. Who was I?

Football was the only thing that remained consistent in my life, so I focused on the game. I thrived in my school's league and continued to thrive for my dad's team. On the field, I wasn't worried about how I talked or the music I listened to–I just wanted to make plays. I found some peace but didn't realize that I was relying on football to numb my identity crisis.

One of the comments that hurt the most was being told that I 'talked white.' I brought this up with my mom, and she said, "First off. There's no such thing as talking white. You speak well." These were words that I wasn't used to hearing. Growing up, I had a speech impediment. While my friends were all having fun at recess in kindergarten and first grade, I was required to take speech therapy classes on the stage in the cafeteria.

When I changed schools in second grade, the other kids laughed at my pronunciation problems. This ignited something within me to become a proficient speaker. Despite the mocking, I would regularly volunteer to read out loud and nominate myself as the speaker in group presentations. When I got home at night, I would stand in front of a mirror and watch myself deliver a speech to a pretend audience of thousands. My disadvantage became a source of motivation to prove I was capable of performing in the classroom just like they were.

In 6th grade, we had a speech competition, and the English teachers chose 8 students from the four English sections in the grade. The final presentation was in front of our parents and the rest of the school. The teacher left it up to us to decide on the topic. I wanted something unique but also something that I was passionate about. I began searching for interesting topics with football and found an article about Naval Academy athletes. It fascinated me that these athletes were required to complete military obligations on top of their academic and athletic requirements. At the time, I didn't even know service academies existed. These athletes were one of a kind. I couldn't wait to present this topic.

I memorized most of my speech for round one. I delivered it confidently and passionately, making eye contact with every student in the room. I was chosen as one of the final 8 and placed in the top 3. That wasn't what stuck with me, though. Following the competition, the father of another finalist pulled me aside and said, "Young man, you have something special inside of you. You're going to inspire many people with your voice one day." I thanked him and stood there in shock as he walked away.

◆ ◆ ◆

As I entered 8th grade, money was getting tight for our family. Jonathan had just left for college, and Nia, Richard, and I were still home. Nia had transferred to a public school, and Richard was in 5th grade at my grandmother's public school. My parents saw this as the perfect opportunity to get our finances back in order. The original plan was for Richard to come and join me at my new private school, but instead, my parents decided it would be best for us to attend our local neighborhood school to catch a break from paying tuition.

New environments promote new growth, though as a kid, I didn't appreciate this much. The first rude awakening was that Richard and I would have to take the bus to school every day. I'm not snobby, but I did enjoy getting dropped off at school by my parents. The second jolt was realizing that I lacked fashion. In private school, I wore a uniform every day. It never crossed my mind to be concerned with the clothes I wore. I just conformed to the people I hung around. The kids at my new school were on a whole different wave.

The first couple of weeks at the new school were rough. I was honestly having a culture shock in an environment I thought I recognized. It was the little things. I was used to doing things on my own time. When I needed to move, I did. Here, we had actual restroom breaks; we lined up, and the teacher walked us to the restroom as a whole class – in complete silence. I couldn't even walk to my next class when the bell rang. We had to "walk the chain," which required us to walk on the outside of the hallway in a circle until we reached our next classroom. This method was supposed to prevent fights–another complete surprise. I hadn't seen one fight in my first eight years in school. That all changed in the second week at my new school. All I remember is sitting in the cafeteria, minding my own business, when suddenly, I felt some wet liquid splash on my back. I turned around to find two girls fighting on the floor. Apparently, one girl walked across the lunchroom and poured milk on the other girl's head. As expected, the other girl didn't appreciate this and stood up to smack the first girl. The first girl pulled the second's hair and slammed her to the ground, punching her victim relentlessly until the security guards came to break it up.

As I looked around, I realized everybody else saw this behavior as normal and expected, but honestly, I was startled. All I could think about was this is not what a school should look like.

In the private school, there was a high emphasis placed on academic success, and teachers gave you the freedom to choose how to accomplish this. At this public school, we were treated like little kids. Everything that we did was monitored and watched. Through a new perspective, I realized that at this new school, the intense control produced a severe backlash when any independent actions were expected. The structure was not designed as a healthy learning environment. My peers felt school was somewhere they were forced to be. They didn't consider it an opportunity to set themselves up for the future. I was ridiculed for wanting to get good grades and for doing my homework. If it weren't for a couple of inspiring teachers, I don't know if I could have maintained my perspective on school.

I was fortunate to find myself in some of the advanced classes. In these classrooms, I encountered some of the smartest people I had ever met. The difference was that these classmates only had some of the resources that my classmates in private school had. They didn't even know what the possibilities were. I knew my experience had produced an uneven playing field, and the unfairness and my privilege were almost embarrassing. Even though I was only in 8th grade, a seed was planted inside of me to help those who might not have access to the obvious resources for success. I wanted them to know, the same way my parents wanted me to know, that you are just as capable as anyone else in the world, given the right tools. Your skin tone isn't a barrier. It is just one component of your identity. It is what is on the inside of you that will allow you to accomplish everything you want in life and more.

In the midst of adjustment, I looked to football to bring me a sense of normalcy, just as I did in private school. My school didn't have a team, so most of the guys there played with a local youth organization participating in the middle school league. I had a close childhood friend who played with another local middle school, so I reached out to him to see if I would be allowed to play on their team. After getting the thumbs up, I arrived at the practice field the next day expecting to make a name for myself.

It was a rough start. I was the smallest player out there. I wasn't the fastest and certainly wasn't the strongest. Before this point, football came naturally. I always felt like I was the guy, and though I was small, my skill level on the field made up for that. I was used to being the star player. From playing in little league and a little private school ball, I knew I would play in the SEC one day and be a first-round draft pick in the NFL. The private school football league stroked my ego. Playing with this middle school team revealed a lot of blind spots for me. The game wasn't coming naturally and didn't give me the confidence I needed as I struggled to find my place in a new environment. I rode the bench that entire season in 8th grade. Although we would go undefeated and win the city championship, I didn't feel I contributed to any of that. All I saw were my inadequacies. All I knew was that I was behind. Much more work needed to be done to achieve my goal of receiving a D1 scholarship one day. It wasn't going to be easy. The question that my dad asked me when I was 5 years old rang in my head: "Who are you going to be?"

2 | THE PROCESS

Jonathan graduated from Christian Brothers High School, and after my 8th-grade year, my parents wanted to send me there to continue the legacy. Everything changed in 2013 when JB's former Head Coach, Kevin Locastro, was recruited by Lausanne Collegiate School (LCS), a school known mostly for academic quality, to build a football program.

After accepting the job at Lausanne, the first thing that Coach Locastro arranged was a meeting with my dad at a local Starbucks. He told my dad, "I just accepted the head coaching job at Lausanne, and I want you to come over there and coach with me." My dad replied, "Lausanne has a football team?" Coach Locastro chuckled and answered, "We do now!!"

My dad told me about the conversation, and my first thought was that no way in the world am I going to be able to play college football if I attended a high school that had never played a down of varsity football. Knowing that I really had no choice, my dad took me to visit Lausanne.

It was weird being back in a private school environment after being in public school for a year. Walking around Lausanne's campus made me feel like I was in an episode of Zoey 101. All of the students seemed joyful and free. I followed my host from class to class, building to building, and took in the culture.

At the end of the visit, I met with the athletic director, Troy Baker. I walked into Coach Baker's office and sat in front of his desk. Baker was an African American man holding degrees from Brown and Vanderbilt University. He was also a straight shooter. I knew he wouldn't feed me a fairytale story. This was a guy who knew how to make things happen. He told me, "Those who come, and stay will become champions. If you come here, you have the opportunity to be a part of something unique. Not everyone can say that they helped build a program. You have the opportunity to be a part of our foundation." That was all I needed to hear. I was sold. I knew, instinctively, that this was bigger than just me. Going to Lausanne would become one of the best decisions that I would make.

◆ ◆ ◆

When I entered the 9th grade, I probably stood around 5 foot 7 inches and generously weighed about 120 pounds soaking wet. If you were to ask anyone at that time what they thought my chances were to play football in college, they would have told you that I had a 100% chance of failure! A guy like me shouldn't have been on a varsity football field that year, but Locastro had to play me because LCS didn't have enough players not to. He shrewdly made me a wide receiver and ran the wishbone. Though compliant, I knew I was just on the field to meet the 11-player requirement. This wasn't the season I envisioned after already having a disappointing 8th-grade year.

My dream of playing in college would take much more effort than I thought. College coaches didn't care who was in your family. They looked at what you could do on the field. No program wanted a 5'7, 120-pound wide receiver. As a matter of fact, I knew that I wasn't going to be a wide receiver anyway because I couldn't catch a cold if you asked me to. My best shot to play at the next level would have to be on the defensive side of the ball – and if I were to do that, I would have to get a lot bigger and stronger.

That off-season, I fell in love with the weight room; I practically lived there. If you know anything about strength coaches, then you know they are some of the craziest coaches on the staff. But our coach, Mark Hamer, might have been a little more than crazy. I remember walking into the weight room, looking at the prescribed workout on the whiteboard, and just wondering, "How in the world did he come up with this?" It was a method behind his madness, though. Every single day, Coach Hamer pushed us beyond our limits with his careful and prudent routine. When we felt like we couldn't do a certain amount of weight, he would tell us to get under the bar, and I learned the principle of mind over matter. If I told my mind I was capable, I usually had a better chance of success. Even if I came up short, I now knew what I needed to do to improve. The worst thing would have been to never try at all.

I made deposits every single day in the weight room.

Some days my motivation was low, my body was sore, and my mind was exhausted. Nevertheless, I showed up. My purpose was bigger than my pain. I promised myself as a kid that my parents wouldn't foot the bill for my higher education. I owed it to them to go earn a scholarship after all their sacrifices. With that as my goal, I didn't need extra incentives. All I had to do was show up and get better.

The discipline I displayed in the weight room and my nutrition plan of hard-boiled eggs in the morning, two-a-day protein shakes, and extra peanut butter and jelly sandwiches at night paid off. After my first off-season, I was able to put on 40 healthy pounds. Despite this growth, I still felt discouraged.

College coaches begin their recruitment during the off-season, and I saw some of my friends garnering their attention. While happy for them, I questioned whether all this work was worth it. I had yet to hear from one school! My discouraged mindset taught me a beautiful lesson: every flower blooms in its own season. Just stay patient, stay committed, and wait for yours.

With my faith as my backbone, I trusted that the football aspect of things would pick up as long as I remained focused. In the meantime, I chose to apply my discipline in the weight room to other areas of my life: academics and leadership.

Lausanne Collegiate School is the top independent school in Memphis and carries a full International Baccalaureate program, one of the most rigorous academic curriculums in the world. As a student, I had the option to enroll in the full IB program or take non-IB classes, which were, honestly, challenging enough. I struggled to maintain good grades on top of my athletics in my freshman and sophomore years. Going into my junior year, it was time to decide whether to take the more challenging full-IB route or simply complete the required courses for graduation. Achieving an IB diploma wasn't something that I needed to do. I was after a football scholarship. However, I understood that life was broader than football. The game would be temporary, but academics would be the key to opening doors of opportunities. The vigorous IB program came with important and far-reaching disciplinary skills. Tools that could help me later down the road. Plus, I always believed that if someone else could do it, I could do it too. I took a deep breath and entered the full IB diploma path–a decision that would serve me well.

Later in my junior year, one lunch conversation led me to another life-changing decision. One day in the springtime, a couple of extra kids joined our usual table. Our conversation was about the upcoming class elections. At the time, Coach Locastro's son was running as the sole candidate for President. Admittedly, he was probably the most popular kid in our grade. He got along with everybody. I made a joke saying something like, "You know what. I'm going to go ahead and run against him to make it interesting." One of my friends that didn't typically sit with us responded, "Now you know good and well you wouldn't be able to beat him." That's all I needed to hear. My competitive nature kicked into full effect.

I announced my candidacy right after lunch. The only actual campaigning that we did was giving an election speech. The whole grade gathered in one of our music rooms to hear the ideas from the candidates for President, Vice President, and Secretary. I knew that a robust and well-delivered speech was essential to swing the election my way. I couldn't make a bunch of promises that I couldn't fulfill, so I spoke about unity. My message was simple: "Together, we can create a legacy for the Class of 2017. How do we want to be remembered?" I directed my attention to the audience, not listing my credentials or achievements. This was a tactic straight from the Bible. When Jesus talked to his disciples, he would compel them to act, not for himself but to further the kingdom of God. The Presidency wasn't about me but about the class and what we would accomplish together. After the speech, my classmates told me they were moved and inspired by my words. I remembered my experience in 6th grade when my friend's parent said, "You're going to inspire a lot of people with your voice one day." I realized that God had just used me to inspire others.

The most unexpected thing happened when the election results came out: there was a tie for President. I wouldn't have wanted it any other way, as I felt honored to be able to share the Presidency. My friend and I came from different backgrounds and hung around different people, but we wanted the same thing: memories to last our class for a lifetime. It worked out perfectly. On top of it all, God had revealed my gift to me again. This time, I suspected there was a more important purpose behind it.

◆ ◆ ◆

Despite my success off the field, I had yet to fulfill my childhood promise. Some other players around the city in my class were starting to receive offers. I didn't let this distract me from my race. I still had the same hunger from my very first off-season. College interest letters were starting to come in, but they were mostly questionnaires. No one was willing to pull the trigger. I knew the right school would call at the right time, though. My older brother always said once you get one offer, the rest will roll in. All I could do was focus on what I had control over and let God handle the rest.

On March 4th, 2016, I was lying on the couch at home and got a call from an unrecognizable 410 area code. I was close to declining it, but something told me to pick it up. It was Coach Ashley Ingram from the United States Naval Academy extending me my first offer to play college football at the Division I level. My promise had been fulfilled. While I was extremely grateful, I really didn't know much about the Academy. My primary connection to the Navy was my grandfather, a retired Navy Chief with over 20 years of service. He always told me about his experiences and all the opportunities the service created for him. I was thankful for the offer, but my eyes were set on a different journey: Vanderbilt. I fell in love with that place ever since I accompanied my sister on a college tour.

A few weeks later, the Vanderbilt coach came by Lausanne. I had high hopes that he would extend me an offer just like Coach Ingram, but it wasn't quite that simple. He told me that they liked what they had seen on film from my junior year, my academics were squared away, and my body frame was indicative of a collegiate corner, but they wanted to see me perform in person. He said if I came to their football camp that summer and performed well, I'd get an offer.

I went to the Vanderbilt camp and had the best football performance of my life. I was making all the right moves, catching one-hand interceptions, snatching the ball away from the receivers, and playing with great technique. I displayed everything you would expect a college coach to want in a 6'2, 185-pound cornerback. It wasn't enough for Vandy, though. I walked away from the camp with no offer.

There were other coaches in attendance. I was already in talks with the coach from Yale, but after seeing me perform at the Vandy camp, he offered me a scholarship on the spot. After news got out about the Yale offer, I received offers from Princeton, UPenn, Harvard, and Columbia. Before I knew it, I had offers from all 8 Ivy League institutions. My drive in the IB curriculum and my dedication on the football field came together to create opportunities that many people dreamed of. A situation I initially viewed as a failure opened the floodgate for new blessings.

As a kid, I remember telling my dad that I would be his first Ivy League football player. I now had the chance to make that statement a reality. Later that summer, I visited some of the Ivy League schools with one of my mentors, a Princeton alumnus himself. I was amazed at the campuses and the prestige that each institution carried. Of all 8, my favorite two were Yale and Princeton. I still wasn't ready to commit, though. Secretly, I felt that if I played well enough in my senior year, then Vanderbilt would swing back around and give me an offer. Besides, I had another lofty goal for my senior year. I wanted to win a state championship.

My senior season was a big year for us. We were on a mission to go undefeated and win the 1st state championship in school history. I wanted to be able to give everything to my team, so I told all the colleges that were recruiting me that I wouldn't focus on my recruitment until after my senior season. This was my last season with my Lausanne brothers.

During my junior season, we got eliminated in the quarterfinals of the state playoffs. However, it was still a lot to celebrate. That season, we finally managed to beat our rival school after being embarrassed by them our first two years. On top of that, we made the playoffs for the first time. Our regular season record was 6-3, and all 3 losses came down to 6 points or less. We traveled to Nashville in the first round of the playoffs to take on a decent opponent and came out victorious. For the next round, we played a team we had already dominated earlier in the regular season, so we felt we had the advantage. With our eyes set on the gold ball, our cockiness slapped us in the face.

Not only did we lose the game, but we were also humiliated. We lost by more than 3 touchdowns. During the fourth quarter, my team was pointing fingers at each other…pointing fingers at the coaches…exactly what the Lausanne culture was NOT supposed to look like. I'm ashamed that I played a role in that. It was a failure on all ends. I specifically remembered the look that our Seniors had, realizing their high school career was over. Some of them just sat on the football field after the clock hit zero. I didn't want to experience any of that pain, and I vowed that if I had anything to do with it, I wouldn't lose a high school game again.

Coach Mario was my position coach at Lausanne. He is the definition of a dreamer. A visionary. His powerful voice often provided motivational speeches throughout moments in practice. While some of them led to laughter due to our immaturity, I appreciated the words that he would share. He spoke success into my life that I didn't believe in until it happened. For Coach Mario, everything was a teachable moment. When he saw our team collapse in the playoffs my junior year, he knew it was a perfect opportunity for us rising seniors to learn the importance of leadership. During that following offseason, he met with us for just this reason.

The last thing that my friends and I wanted to do was get up at 7 AM on a Saturday in the off-season and go listen to these hour-long talks about leadership. However, Coach Mario knew we needed to be groomed. We had to grow ourselves first before we could inspire growth in others. As a group, we identified what we wanted our end goal to be (state championship), and then we identified key values of a championship team to implement into our program. We challenged ourselves with 5 AM workouts in the off-season to demonstrate the importance of work ethic to the guys below us. We handled our business in the classroom and stayed out of trouble with the teachers. Leading by example would be key to getting the younger players to buy in, so we could accomplish something that had yet to be done at Lausanne. We knew that success wouldn't just fall into our lap. We had to go create it. Every single day, we challenged ourselves to get uncomfortable. Not because we wanted to but because we needed to. One of the most reused success quotes you hear nowadays is, "If you want to be successful, then you have to be willing to do the things that others don't want to do." While I agree with that quote, the truth is...it's not about others. It's a battle against yourself. It's about what *you* don't want to do.

Every game that year, we set out to dominate our opponent. We didn't care who we played. We were on a mission to make a statement, and whatever team we met was in the way. We took every single game week to week.

We held each other accountable on and off the field. We even documented the season on YouTube because we knew our team was about to do something special. (Check out YMWI: The Crew) But, most importantly, we had fun and created memories.

On December 1st, 2016, after just 4 years of being a varsity program, we reaped the benefits of our sacrifices as we captured Lausanne's first football state championship and finished the season with a record of 14-0. The measure of change wasn't just temporary, though. Lausanne would go on to become ranked top 50 in the country and win 38 games in a row before falling in the state semifinals in 2018, creating the longest winning streak in the history of Memphis high school football.

By the time I wrapped up my senior season, I was a 2-star athlete with more than 15 Division I offers. You would think I would be happy, but truth be told, I was still a little bitter. I still didn't have that Vanderbilt offer. I felt slighted and dismissed. If I could go back to that senior-year-Cameron, I would shake him. Literally. I lost sight of how far I had come since that freshman wide receiver who had no shot at playing in college. The absence of a Vanderbilt scholarship did not define me–all I needed was one opportunity. One that I had worked my butt off to earn. A full-ride scholarship to any level collegiate program is rare. Only 9% of high school football players get to play in college. If you're going D-1, even better. You're a part of 2.8%. You're blessed. Thinking any other way is selfish, immature, and unproductive. I couldn't neglect the blessings I had right in front of me.

As signing day approached, I narrowed the list down to 4 schools and scheduled official visits to all of them: Air Force, Princeton, Yale, and Navy. I visited the Air Force

Academy first, and I liked the school a lot. I had never been to Colorado before, and the mountains in Colorado Springs were breathtaking. Sadly, I suddenly grasped that I didn't want to be that far away from home without any family, knowing that my parents wouldn't be able to make many games. Plus, I wanted to be around a little bit of city life.

Princeton was my second visit, and I was planning on committing. However, something didn't feel right when I got to New Jersey. I wasn't comfortable. Princeton was prestigious, but I didn't think I would get the development I wanted and needed. After that visit, I decided I didn't want to go to an Ivy League school, so I canceled my visit to Yale. That left one last visit: the United States Naval Academy.

I was nervous. Signing day was a week away, and I still had no idea where I was going. If I didn't like the Naval Academy, the next step was unclear. I asked my older brother, Jonathan, how he knew Illinois was the school for him. His response was, "You'll know. It's a feeling that I can't explain." Not a big help. It wasn't the answer I needed.

I landed in Annapolis, MD on the last weekend of January 2017, asking God to reveal His next plans for my life. I hoped to get an answer, even if this visit didn't bear fruit. We were picked up in a black SUV from the Baltimore-Washington airport by Coach Ingram. We entered Annapolis by a bridge that overlooked the entire campus. I gazed outside my window and admired the famous grounds bathing in the sunlight. The water complimented the campus perfectly. It was beautiful and like nothing I had ever seen before. At that moment, before I even stepped foot into the school, I knew that's where I would spend the next 4 years of my life. Jonathan was right, and so was God's plan.

3 | THE SCRIPTURE

Midshipmen must reflect on the fact that we are officers in training. Our college experience consists of more than just academics and athletics. We're preparing to be officers in the United States Navy and the United States Marine Corps. This isn't something that you can just wake up and do. You must be groomed into the standards of being an officer. This starts on Day 1 at the Academy. A day that is known as "Induction Day," marking the beginning of Plebe Summer. There would be no football activity for a month.

As I lay in my hotel bed, excited but nervous about the new journey ahead, I had butterflies in my stomach the night before I-Day. I rolled over to look at my parents, who were sleeping in the other bed in our hotel room. To my surprise, my dad was still sitting in a chair, writing a letter. He could tell that I was a little restless. "God has His hands on you," he said. "This is all a part of His plan. You're going to be alright. I'm proud of you." Those words provided me with a sense of peace and enough comfort to close my eyes and get some rest before the next chapter of my life began.

Induction Day at the Naval Academy can be summed up in one word: chaos. There was a lot of yelling, which I didn't mind because I was used to my coaches yelling. However, something about getting yelled at by people only a few years older than me didn't sit right. These detailers were the upperclassmen. While basic training was for the incoming Plebes, the upperclassmen were in training, too. They were testing leadership styles and techniques learned from their earlier years at the Academy, sometimes remembering the harsh treatment they received.

We stood in line for hours in the blazing heat, waiting to enter Alumni Hall, the Academy's basketball arena. Once I finally got to the front of the line, I hugged my parents and walked through the doors, knowing that if I embraced them too long, emotions would overtake me. After hours of paperwork, medical clearance, and uniform distribution, I made the hike from Alumni Hall to the 3rd floor of the 5th wing of our dormitory, Bancroft Hall. I found myself standing on the bulkhead (fancy military word for wall), getting yelled at by one of my new detailers. He kept asking me what the mission of the Naval Academy was, and I kept telling him that I didn't know. He wanted me to say: "I'll find out, sir." Rather than telling me what he wanted, the detailer continued to yell until one of my classmates finally whispered the proper response to me. Interactions like this continued for hours. My head spun in circles all day until it finally came time for lights out. As I lay in my rack that first night at the Academy, I stared at the ceiling, wondering what in the world I had gotten myself into.

My first couple weeks of basic training were spent trying to impress the detailers. I figured they would lay off me a little bit if I could get them to like me–a massive mistake on my end. It didn't matter how clean I thought my uniform was, how many pushups I could do, or how many rates I could memorize; there was always something that could be done better. More importantly, this carried negative connotations for the rest of my squad if they, too, weren't doing well. It took me a minute to figure this out because I forgot I was part of a team.

Once, our squad leader was taking us through a physical training (PT) session after being disappointed that all but one of us knew "the Qualifications of a Naval Officer." He had us all get down in a high plank position and recite the 5th law of the Navy together:

"On the strength of one link in the cable, dependeth the might of the chain. Who knows when thou may'st be tested, so live that thou bearest the strain."

We were only as strong as our weakest link.

I never minded the physical activity. I was a Division 1 football player, for Heaven's sake. If I couldn't handle some basic PT, then I had no business stepping on a collegiate football field. However, during this session, I saw my squad mate struggle significantly to stay in a plank position. She kept falling and shaking to stay up. Our detailer loved every minute of it. He got in her face encouraging her to just quit and give up. As the yelling increased and the PT continued, tears began falling down her face. At that moment, I felt selfish. I was the weakest link. I placed my right hand inside her left hand so she could use my shoulder to support her to stay up. Once our squad leader saw this, he ceased the PT session. Right then, I realized the significance of basic training: it's bigger than you. Basic training was structured to tear you down before the detailers build you back up. The Naval Academy recruits the cream of the crop: valedictorians, class presidents, team captains, Eagle Scouts, etc. When you get to campus, you are full of yourself. It wasn't about us as individuals, though. It was about becoming a part of a much greater team. There's no room for ego.

◆ ◆ ◆

I had to switch gears when the time finally came to begin football training camp. In those weeks of basic training, I still had not lost sight of my goal for that season. I had my eyes laser-focused on October 14th, 2017, when we were scheduled to travel to Memphis to take on the Tigers.

On average, about 4-5 freshmen out of a class of around 50 make the travel roster in their first season. When you're up against those odds, the key is standing out early. Knowing that it would take a couple of weeks for my skills to get back to where I needed them to be, I didn't have time to wait on my talent. My advantage would have to come from my work ethic and earning the coaches' trust. It takes little skill to be coachable. All you need is some humility and discipline. Fortunately, my parents had already instilled this in me as a young man.

When I walked into the cornerback meeting room for our first meeting, I immediately noticed the big board. It had the whole defensive depth chart, every position, every player. I saw my name as the 5th left corner. There were 4 corners listed on the right side, so this meant I was 9 out of 9. At most, 6 corners would travel, requiring me to beat out at least 3 upperclassmen. The upperclassmen had spent the whole summer in our lifting and conditioning program and had played in the same system in the previous years, so they already knew the plays. More importantly, our coach already knew their names. I couldn't focus on that, though. There was nothing that I could do about the depth chart. There was nothing I could do about the upperclassmen. All I could do was control my work ethic and attitude. If I looked in the mirror at the end of each day of training camp and could say I gave my all, I knew God would handle the rest.

I committed to understanding the playbook better than anyone in the position room. If I made a mistake in practice, I ensured that I made the error at full speed. I did my best to learn from the coach's pointers, so I didn't make the same mistake twice. I showed up first to our meetings. I asked questions to show that I was engaged. After a few weeks, I worked my way up into the top six. As we entered the final week of training camp, our coach told us that only the 1st four corners had secured a spot on the travel roster. Everybody else was on the cusp of traveling or playing scout team. It would all come down to special teams.

Special teams aren't very glorious and often get overlooked unless a game-changing play takes place. The special teams period usually occurred in the middle of our practices when you were dog-tired. Many guys saw this as a time to catch their breath from individual or team drills. However, I saw this as an opportunity to catch one of the four special teams' coaches' eyes so I could slide my way into the depth chart. I gave everything I had every single rep. When I wasn't going, I watched the other guys to learn from their mistakes. My attention to detail would serve me well. By the end of training camp, I was on two of the special teams' depth charts, which solidified my spot on the travel roster. My goal was accomplished.

◆ ◆ ◆

After 5 weeks into the season, the moment finally came for us to travel to take on the Memphis Tigers. I felt good heading into the game against Memphis. In those 5 weeks prior, I saw action on kickoff and recorded some of my first college football tackles. It was my first trip back to the city since I left for basic training in June. 30 family members were coming to the game, as well as former teammates, former coaches, and former classmates…it was my time to put on a show.

Our defense had finally forced a 4th down in the 3rd quarter of the game, which meant it was time for me to get my first piece of the action on punt return. I hadn't played punt return that season, but my role was like playing cornerback. My objective was to keep the gunner on the punt team from having a direct path to our punt returner. I needed to force him outside to buy our returner time to catch and advance the football. I sprinted across the turf at the Liberty Bowl with a smile on my face. I lined up in front of my opponent, took a deep breath, and waited for his first move, indicating the ball had been snapped. He gave me a quick jab to the inside, and I hopped over to defend him from beating me inside, but to my surprise, he turned to take the outside lane and morphed into Usain Bolt. I found myself in a trail position very quickly – by 10-

15 yards. At that moment, I knew I had just fumbled the opportunity I had been preparing and praying for. The lights were too big for me.

When I returned to school that Monday after the game, my coach texted me and told me to meet him in his office before practice. My stomach dropped. You know that feeling when your mama calls you, and you just know you're in trouble? Even if you don't see what you did wrong? I knew I had messed up. When I got to his office, he asked how my family was and how school was going. Then he asked how I thought the game went last week. "It was definitely not high school," I said. "The speed of the game was faster, but I felt like it was a good taste. There are definitely some areas where I could improve."

"Cam, we feel like you have a lot of potential," he started. Right then, I knew this wasn't going to be good. "One day, you'll make big plays for this program. But we don't think you're there right now. You don't have the speed. You're too tight in your hips to play cornerback at this level. We need to see improvement in those areas, so I'm moving you to the scout team for the rest of the season." This was common at the Academy. Guys got moved up and down from scout team to varsity all the time, but I was distraught and embarrassed. I was about to go from being a high school state champion to holding bags in practice: What kind of road to glory was this?

After the meeting, I immediately called my dad. It was time for another "Father-Coach to Son-Player" conversation. I told him the story and that I honestly didn't know if I wanted to continue playing. He cut me off right there. "You're looking at the situation from the wrong perspective, son. Focus on the deficiencies the coach mentioned, so you can come back better and compete next season." He was right.

When I returned to my room, I opened a container that held all my letters from basic training. I was looking for the first letter I read, one from my dad, the same one he was writing when we were in the hotel room the night before I-Day. The letter had a scripture that would become a staple in my life: Jeremiah 29:11.

> *"For I know the plans I have for you," declares the LORD, "plans to prosper you and not to harm you, plans to give you hope and a future." (NIV)*

As a part of God's plan for my life, I knew the Academy would provide me with the preparation I needed to become the man God needed me to be. I read that scripture and realized that His plan wouldn't always be sunshine and rainbows. There would be dark times, and God is still with us in these dark times. Jeremiah 29:11 reminds us that God has plans to prosper and not harm us. Plans that provide us with hope and a future. I asked myself the same question I was asked at the age of 5, "Who are you going to be?" I could quit, or I could embrace this situation and become a better man and player because of it.

My dad always told me that I would find out if I really loved the game of football when I got to college. The weeks I spent on the scout team at the Naval Academy showed me what he meant. I'm a team player and willing to do whatever it takes to help my team be successful. However, I refused to be defined or labeled as a scout team player. I approached practice on the scout team the way I would've approached practice if I were the starting cornerback. I didn't take it easy on our offense. I fought off blocks. I made plays on the ball. I ran to the football to tag off. The only thing I wouldn't do was come near the quarterback–you never go near the quarterback.

Part of the growth process is knowing the things you specifically need. You must have the humility to look honestly in the mirror and recognize your weaknesses. Once you're aware of the weaknesses, you can take steps to pour energy into those areas to see improvement. I recalled my coach's feedback in our meeting: "You don't have the speed right now... You're too tight in your hips to play cornerback at this level." Speed and flexibility. Those were the two areas that I would attack relentlessly.

For my flexibility, I dedicated 30 minutes in the morning and 30 minutes at night to a stretching routine of foam rolling, resistance band, and static stretching. This was the same routine that I maintained during track season when I was in high school. I've always felt like my body was in peak condition when running track, so it could help me out in my current circumstances. I knew I would need more than that little exercise routine, though. My answers came from the yoga club at the Naval Academy.

I didn't know anyone in the yoga club. I felt extremely out of place as a stiff football player in a room full of majestic mindfulness. I just came in with my mat, went to the back of the room, and did what I could to get more flexible. I thought yoga was supposed to be peaceful, but it was painful. However, after weeks and weeks of consistency, I could feel a difference in my body. Sticking through the uncomfortableness allowed me to experience growth in a weak area.

This flexibility would only solve some of my issues; I also needed to improve on the field. But time was limited, and I needed to ensure my grades stayed up to par. The only other option would be before school. I decided to get up at 5:30 in the morning, 3 days a week, and head to Halsey Field House. During these workout sessions, I would go through various drills that I found on YouTube and Instagram. While going through these workouts, I often looked around the fieldhouse to see I was the only one there. No eyes, no cameras...just me. I would simulate game situations while doing the drills and visualize myself making big plays in Navy-Marine Corps Stadium. I was instilling belief in myself and speaking into existence the future success I could have as a football player.

Failure isn't a setback; it's just the tool you need to move forward. Your perspective of failure changes the effects of failure. There is always opportunity in adversity. When I moved to the scout team, I thought my football career was over. That's because I had yet to see my failure as an opportunity to grow.

That next season, I worked my way into the rotation. In fact, I was even able to start a couple of games. I felt like a new ball player, and it felt good. With more playing time, I also made more mistakes. These errors would impact my confidence tremendously, especially if I was pulled from the game. I needed to be more consistent. I kept telling myself Jeremiah 29:11. Whether the game was good or bad, Jeremiah 29:11. Everything was a part of God's plan. I had to remember that He was working for my good.

◆ ◆ ◆

With the inconsistency in football, I started to look for other ways to get involved at the Academy. Around the midpoint in the season, we got an email saying that class elections were open for Class President, Vice President,

Secretary, and Treasurer. I was intrigued by the opportunity. I enjoyed serving as Co-Class President during my senior year in high school, so this would be a great chance to get to know my classmates. I was nervous about my chances of winning, so I called my mother to tell her about the opportunity.

"Well, are you going to do it?" She asked.
"Honestly," I started. "I don't know if I can win. I barely know anybody other than my teammates."
"If that's the only thing holding you back, then you know what to do," She responded.

Fear. Fear. Fear. There is a poem that goes, "Fear is a little mind killer that disintegrates me from the inside out. I must learn to face it and control it."

Everybody desires to grow, develop, and become something more, but fear will prevent you from even going after an opportunity that could change your life. My mom was essentially telling me that I couldn't let fear be the only thing that held me back from putting my name in the hat. She was right. I needed to go after the presidential position. However, in my days of hesitation for running, one of my teammates announced his candidacy for Class President. I didn't want to conflict with voting, so I decided to run as Vice President.

Candidates were to create a one-page bio sheet with a picture. This bio sheet was then dropped in a Google Drive with the bios from the other candidates. The folder was shared with the entire grade, and an email was sent out with a poll for each person to nominate a candidate for each position. The administrators would then take the top 5 candidates for President and Vice-president and the top

3 for Secretary and Treasurer. These final candidates would be allowed to give speeches to the class before the last election polls opened.

There were about 30 candidates for Vice President. If I could make it out of the bio sheet round, I would have a good chance of swaying over voters during my speech. In my mind, that was a big "if." Bio sheets were simply a popularity contest and name recognition. I only knew a few people in my grade, so I didn't like my chances. When the results came out from the first polls, I saw my name in the 5th position. I had barely made the cut, but I made it.

I centered my speech around unity and started with a quote from my mother: "We might not have it all together, but together, we have it all." Throughout the speech, I explained that we all have a role to play in the class of 2021. We might come from different backgrounds and have come to the Academy for various reasons, but we were all midshipmen. If we wanted the best experience as a class, we would need to appreciate our differences and the unique qualities they brought to our academy family.

After the speech, my inbox was flooded with emails from classmates. When the voting came out, I won by a landslide. God's gift paved the way for me again. That next year, I got promoted to Class President, and, in response, my mother reminded me, "What God has for you is for you." I just hoped some success on the football field was also in His plans.

4 | THE STORM

Our program decided to go in a different direction after finishing the season with a 3-10 record. Our Head Coach, Ken Niumatalolo, brought in an entirely new defensive staff. With a clean slate, I saw this as the perfect opportunity to lock down a starting role. I followed a similar off-season plan from the previous year but placed a lot more emphasis on my mental growth. During my sophomore season, I struggled with confidence as I often worried that making a mistake would get me pulled out of the game. However, I knew playing with fear prevented me from reaching my full potential. I had to believe in myself first if I expected the coaches to also believe in me.

Going into my junior year, I finally locked down the starting job. In the first game of the season against Holy Cross, I earned our team's defensive player of the week. The momentum continued to build throughout the season. The biggest highlight was making a game-sealing pass deflection against #24-ranked SMU to help our team get the win on senior night. We went 11-2 that year and finished #23 in the country. We won the Commander-In-Chief trophy after beating both Army and Air Force and finished the year off by beating Kansas State in the Auto-Zone Liberty Bowl in Memphis, TN on New Year's Eve. I finally got a chance to redeem myself from my poor performance in my freshman year. My confidence took a leap as I started all 13 games and, for the most part, saw drastic improvements from my first two years. For the first time since being in college, I went into the off-season proud. Little did I know, 2020 was about to take the world by storm.

After leaving school for spring break, we never returned. The Covid-19 pandemic was making its presence known across the world. This gave me a lot of quality time at home with my family and a lot of time for reflection. I knew senior year meant that a new chapter of my life was about to begin. It'd be my last year playing football, and I needed to figure out what was next for my military career. I was excited but nervous at the same time. Near the end of June, we finally got the go-ahead to return to the Academy.

The drive from Memphis to Annapolis was around 13 hours. I had already made this trip several times, a couple of times joined by friends, but a few times on my own. I dreaded the drive in the past because it meant it was time to go back to school. Due to the unique circumstances, I was excited about this 13-hour journey because it meant that football was finally about to resume. I was on the home stretch of the drive with about 4 hours remaining. Most of the drive was blessed with clear weather, but I noticed a little sprinkling fall from the sky. As I was coming around a bend on the highway, I felt my car shake slightly.

    I attempted to stabilize the vehicle, and within seconds, I swerved uncontrollably on the highway. I didn't begin to panic just yet. I eased my foot off the gas, and suddenly, I found myself spinning in circles down the highway: panic button pressed. I looked out the left side of my car and saw that if my momentum didn't stop, I'd be carried right off a cliff. On the right side, I saw an 18-wheeler coming in my direction. Either way, I knew that this was possibly it for me. My life was no longer in my hands. As the 18-wheeler got closer, I closed my eyes and extended my arms for impact. "Lord, I thank you" were the last words to leave my mouth. In my mind, I saw pictures flashing from when I was a little kid until now.

BOOM.

After making contact with the 18-wheeler, my 2015 Dodge Challenger was tossed into the railing on the side of the highway. I opened my eyes and realized that I was still alive. I began recounting the events that just took place, when the next thing I knew, a crowd was running to the car. Once they got to my vehicle, they slammed on the window until I opened my car door. "Omg, omg, are you ok??" "How are you alive??" "Do you need us to call the ambulance??" I could see that they were honestly shocked to even see me breathing and unharmed. The only thing on my mind was that my beloved car was totaled. I had just gotten it a new paint job a few weeks before. The matte black exterior complimented the car's black rims and red interior seats. Honestly, I idolized that car. I finally made my way out of the vehicle and called my mother to let her know what happened.

"Hey, Mom. I just got into a bad car accident," I told her.
"Oh my goodness, are you okay?? What happened?? Where are you??" I could tell she was panicking.
"Everything is fine, Mom," I reassured her. "I hydroplaned and got hit by an 18-wheeler, but I'm fine. I'm in Virginia, about four hours away from Maryland. My car is totaled though, Mom. My car is gone."
"Baby, your car is replaceable. Your life isn't," she said, sobbing through the phone.

Upon hearing that last sentence, I broke down crying on the side of the highway. My mom was right. I was lucky to be alive. I walked away from that accident without a scratch on my body. God protected my life and taught me a lesson in the process. He was preparing me for a year of more loss.

◆ ◆ ◆

I had a lot of high expectations as I headed into my senior year. I knew this would be my last season playing football, and I wanted to go out with a bang. At the Naval Academy, only two positions are chosen by your peers: class office positions and team captains. My teammates named me as one of our three team captains, so I now held both, all glory to God.

The season started off on a rough note. Due to the pandemic, our game in Ireland against the Notre Dame Fighting Irish had been canceled. Instead, we were playing BYU on Labor Day on ESPN, the only college football game on T.V. that day. Everybody knew the name Zach Wilson after what happened to us. We lost that game 55-3. The following week, we played against Tulane. We saw this as an opportunity to bounce back but quickly found ourselves down 24-0 midway through the second quarter. Right before the half, Tulane was driving to score again. I baited the quarterback into thinking I would jump a short route, causing him to float a deep ball right into my arms for my first collegiate interception. It was a sigh of relief.

In the locker room at halftime, I had a strange feeling that everything would be okay. Much of that was due to my mindfulness coach, Dr. Greg Graber. Before the season, I received a copy of his mindfulness book. In one chapter, there was a breathing exercise called "Faith over Fear." In this exercise, you breathe in through your nose for 3 seconds, saying the word "faith" in your head. You hold your breath for 3 seconds, then exhale through your mouth for 3 seconds, saying the word "fear." It fills you up with faith, eliminating the fear from your body. The technique kept me grounded and pressure-free. We went out in the second half, led by my guy Dalen Morris at QB, and completed the largest comeback in Navy football history, defeating Tulane 27-24.

Momentum was back headed into the Air Force game, and we got smashed. We were now 1-2. I felt like I was failing as a leader. The conditions at the Academy were already rough. The last thing you wanted to throw on top of that was a losing season. Winning was the only thing that could make our situation better. After our workout on Monday following the Air Force game, I called the team together. I expressed my embarrassment from getting beat by 30 by our service academy rival. I promised to hold everybody accountable and to set an example myself. I knew we were a better team than what we had been displaying thus far.

We responded well, rattling off two wins against Temple and ECU. At the season half-way point, we had a 3-2 record. Not bad, but not good either. My position coach called me into his office midway through the week, heading into our game against Houston. He was my third position coach since I had been at the Academy. All of my coaches brought value into my life. My first coach taught me the importance of growth, and he brought a lot of passion to the game. My second coach helped me grow in my faith and use that as fuel to play the game of football. This third coach was one of the realest I've encountered. He didn't treat us like we were his players or his sons. He treated us like grown men. He almost felt like a big brother to me. When he called me in to meet, I figured it would be a check-up on life.

"I called you in here to let you know that we'll be rolling with a different look this week. You won't be starting. I don't want this to discourage you, but we want to give some other guys a look."

"Here we go again," I thought. I felt the same way from my freshman year. I had been playing on an even keel that season. In a few moments, I looked like an all-conference corner; in others, I looked like a guy who shouldn't be on a Division I football field. My confidence was building, though, as I had just come off of a strong performance against ECU. I had three pass breakups, including two big fourth-down stops. On top of that, I had just been named a finalist for the William V. Campbell Trophy, otherwise known as the Academic Heisman. I was trending in the right direction for sure.

Feelings don't matter in college football. It's a business. You must respect the aspect of the business because these coaches are getting paid for what they do. If you don't perform, their jobs are on the line. As a result, they must make decisions to get the best eleven on the field. If you want to be on the field, you better find a way to be one of those best eleven, and I still felt like I was one of those best eleven. I was sick, frustrated, angry, disappointed, embarrassed. Everything.

As team captain, I worried I would lose my credibility as a leader. I literally just promised to set the example and now I was losing my starting role. I was a letdown. My teammates placed trust in someone they respected, not a bench rider. Who wants to listen to somebody that isn't even in the game? I gave myself a few days to sit with my emotions, but I knew I couldn't stay there forever. I found myself asking the same question that my dad asked me at age 5, "Who are you going to be?"

I still remember watching the T.V. copy of the Houston game in my dorm room, my first time not starting after 18 straight games. The broadcast zoomed in to me standing on the sideline at a point in the game. "There is Cameron Kinley. Class President and team captain. Not making his first start in 18 games." Humiliation. Why single me out? I closed the YouTube browser and googled scriptures for persevering through hard times. I came across the scripture of James chapter 1, specifically verses 2-4 and verse 12:

> *"2 Consider it pure joy, my brothers and sisters, whenever you face trials of many kinds, 3 because you know that the testing of your faith produces*

perseverance. 4 Let perseverance finish its work so that you may be mature and complete, not lacking anything...12 Blessed is the one who perseveres under trial because, having stood the test, that person will receive the crown of life that the Lord has promised to those who love him." (NIV)

Perspective is everything. James tells us that a difficult situation is a blessing because it produces perseverance. And why is perseverance good? Because it makes you complete. In verse 12, he explains further, *"Blessed is the one who perseveres under trial...."* Hard times are not a burden. God is preparing you; the worst thing that could happen is not being ready to accept God's blessing. Losing my job was preparation for something bigger. I trusted that God was molding me.

Things didn't get easier as the season went on. Unanticipated circumstances caused me to start the next two games. The first was against SMU because one of our guys had a concussion, and the second was because we were playing against the University of Memphis, my hometown. Both games were challenging as I felt I had something to prove rather than just going out there to enjoy the game I loved. Against Memphis, I started the game and played the first series. I was subbed out the very next series. Memphis drove down the field in that series and got inside our 20-yard line. One of our corners lost a shoe, so my coach threw me into the game. I was matched up man to man against one of my high school rivals and now friend, Calvin Austin III. During the week, I watched a lot of film on Calvin and knew that he tended to push the corner outside, fake inside, then come back out at the end of his route. I saw the exact alignment I saw on film, he pushed outside on the snap, so I kept outside leverage, expecting him to break right into me. Instead of coming out, Calvin broke off to the inside, where the ball fell right into his hands for a touchdown. That would be my last play for the rest of the game.

I'd argue that cornerback is the most challenging position in football. It's unforgiving. You can play well the whole game, get beat once, and everybody will think you're the worst player. Every mistake you make at that position will likely result in a big play. You can't beat yourself up about it, though. You must have short-term memory. You have to keep playing like the greats do—next-play mentality. While I didn't get my next play in that game, I took that lesson for my next play in life.

Despite my spirits being down, I showed up to every practice ready to work. Realizing that my playing days were nearly behind me, I helped coach up the guys who were now ahead of me. It was challenging to do this. I felt like I was the better player, but I swallowed my pride and contributed to the team in any way I could.

I wish I could say I was the positive, inspiring guy every day, but I wasn't. It was painful as I watched my career fade away. I spent hours talking to some of my coaches back home and venting to some of my other teammates. It wasn't a fair situation to me. But like my mama always used to say, "Life ain't fair."

♦ ♦ ♦

Our last game of the regular season every year was always the biggest one: Army. The Army-Navy game is a battle between our future leaders and military members in front of 70,000 passionate fans who understand the commitment that each athlete has already sworn to make. It is by far the greatest experience that college football has to offer. It's bigger than a rivalry. This year was different, though. Due to Covid-19, we couldn't play the game at a neutral site, which required us to travel to West Point to play Army in their home stadium. This was the first time it had been held at West Point since World War II. The game-day forecast matched West Point's campus' dull, gray walls. If you were watching on T.V., you could barely even see the game due to the thick layers of fog.

My record against Army heading into that game was 1-2. I didn't play my first two years, but I finally got to experience what the game was like my junior year when we snapped Army's 3-year winning streak. I hoped to get a chance to contribute to this 2020 game, but given the past few weeks, I knew these chances were slim. Nevertheless, I still wanted to end my football career on a high note with a win over our long-time rivals.

I went out for the coin toss, where I was met at the 50-yard line by the President of the United States, President Trump, at the time. Regardless of how you feel about President Trump, being within 3 ft of the POTUS was an unreal experience. It almost felt like I was breaking the law being that close to him. I called tails in the air and won the coin toss for probably the 3rd time that season. After shaking hands with Army's captain, I returned to our sideline. That was the last time I touched the field until the fourth quarter.

The Army-Navy game is typically low-scoring. We both know what plays the other team will run since both schools have the same offenses. The game ultimately depends on who wins the turnover battle and wants it more. We went into halftime down 3-0 and quickly saw that deficit change to 15-0 early in the 4th quarter. A harsh reality was starting to kick in.

With a little more than a minute left in the game, I finally got to see some action. Well, I don't know if the word "action" accurately depicts it. It was three plays. The memory is so vivid. The Black Knights had just taken a knee for the game's final play, and we all watched the last seconds tick off the scoreboard. To spectators and players, it signified the end of the game, meaning that Army had just beaten us for the 4th time in 5 years. For me, those seconds ticking off the clock signified the end of my football career.

Walking across the field after the game, I was numb to the Army players celebrating and the screaming Army fans. I was even numb to the small skirmish that broke out between the two teams after the game. I was in my own world. Had I really just played my last football game? Seventeen years of my life were dedicated to this sport. It's no way that a 17-year journey was supposed to end like this.

My career didn't have to be over. There was always the option of the NFL, where I could continue playing football at the highest level and fulfill a childhood dream. However, I didn't have the accolades, and the odds weren't in my favor. I wasn't an all-conference guy. I had just lost my starting job as a senior. So, there was one problem: I didn't think I was good enough. I was scared of failing. I feared what other people would say. It can be harmful when you let the opinions of others dictate what you're capable of achieving because it damages your perception of possibilities. When I was a kid, nobody could tell me that I wasn't going to the NFL. I didn't care what anybody else had to say. As I got older, the opinions of others started to have a direct impact on how I viewed my football capabilities. Truth be told, when I got to the Naval Academy, I wasn't thinking about the NFL anymore because I didn't think I could make it. I thought my college career would satisfy all I craved with the game of football. However, that fairytale didn't have the perfect ending, leaving me wanting more.

I eventually made my way off the field and into the locker room at Michie Stadium. My dad had told me his story about his last college football game against Boise State. He remembered how he took his pads off slowly, knowing he would never put them on again. I now sat in the locker room of Michie Stadium feeling as he had. I took my time unbuckling my shoulder pads before slowly sliding them over my head. Holding back the tears, I sat there with my face in my hands. I was honestly in disbelief. "There's no way this can be it," I thought. I kept returning to the fact that I wasn't good enough to make it to the NFL. The fear of putting myself out there and failing to achieve my dreams nearly choked me.

When I got on the bus after the game, I got a call from one of my mentors. He asked me why I didn't play in the game, and I just let him know that I wasn't a part of the defensive game plan for that week. His response caught me off guard: "Well, I guess it's time to get ready for the NFL now." I laughed it off and asked, "Do you really think I could make it to the NFL? I barely played the second half of my senior season. Teams don't want a guy like that." He reassured me, saying, "If you produce good pro-day results, then there's no way a team wouldn't take a shot on you." I still wasn't sold, though

5 | THE LEAP

Once I finally got back home to Memphis, I felt like a weight was lifted from my shoulders. I hadn't been home since leaving for school in June. After the way the season went and dealing with Covid-19, opening the door and smelling the Kinley household again eased my heart. At the same time, my mentor's comments still rang in my head.

My family always enjoyed working out in the garage over winter break. Richard and I were always there, and my dad occasionally joined us. We were out there one day getting it in, and after my final bench press rep, I turned and asked Richard, "Do you think I should try to go to the NFL?" "If you're asking me that, then you already know the answer," he responded.

One thing about my little brother Richard is that he always keeps it real with me. He's practically my best friend. After Nia graduated from high school, it was just

Richard and me in the house with our parents for my last two years at Lausanne. We got extremely close and knew each other well during that time. Richard had a front-row seat to my growth as a player, so I knew he would be honest with me. My dad was there to clarify what Richard meant. "Till this day, I still wish I would've gone after the opportunity. I didn't have all the accolades or stats, either. You don't want to live with the 'What if?' syndrome for the rest of your life."

My little brother retorted, "But if you say you're going to do it, then you have to commit to it. You can't be playing around and not be locked in. You got a lot of work to do. If anyone can make it happen, though, it's you." My little brother didn't realize it, but at that moment, he became a part of my inspiration for the journey. Richard's belief in me motivated me to show him it was possible.

Though the odds were against me, I wanted to chase my dream of playing football in the NFL. They say less than 1% of football players accomplish this. As for me, I was a 2-star recruit coming out of high school, never made all-conference in college, and didn't even start the second half of my senior season. I had a better chance of getting struck by lightning or winning the lottery than playing in the NFL. But I knew I couldn't live the rest of my life asking, "What if?". All I could do was create a perception of possibility to believe my dream could come true.

To hold myself accountable, I announced publicly that I was declaring for the NFL draft. This was a big step for me in overcoming my fears: the fear of failure, the fear of judgment, and the fear of not being enough.

My post's caption was *"Walk by faith, not by sight,"* 2 Corinthians 5:7. Stepping out on faith and betting on yourself and your strength can sometimes be scary. In

Hebrews 11:1 (NIV), Paul defines faith: *"Now faith is confidence in what we hope for and assurance about what we do not see."* Two words stick out to me: "confidence" and "assurance." You cannot have faith without confidence. You cannot have faith without assurance. You must believe in what you're asking God for. You must expect that your requests will be fulfilled. Even though you may only see the partial picture right now, you must have the assurance that the full picture is more beautiful than anything you've ever experienced. Even if it's not the result that you were expecting. God's plan for you is perfect. You must be confident of that. Paul continues, *"By faith Abraham, when called to go to a place he would later receive as his inheritance, obeyed and went, even though he did not know where he was going."* Abraham had faith despite having complete knowledge. I was walking in this faith. I wanted to show the world what is possible when God controls the wheel. I was about to embark on a journey that demonstrated the value of placing faith over fear.

◆ ◆ ◆

God started working immediately. The NFL combine was canceled in 2021 due to Covid-19. This left NFL prospects scrambling to find any way to get seen in front of scouts. The College Gridiron Showcase was one of these opportunities. Within the first week of declaring for the draft, I signed with an agent and got invited to the Showcase. There were multiple athletes with combine invites, Senior Bowl, NFLPA Collegiate Bowl, and many more. The College Gridiron Showcase was my sole opportunity to get noticed by one of the 32 NFL teams.

Identity

The Showcase was a two-day event: Day 1 for measurements and interviews and Day 2 for on-field work. Near the end of day 1, they had all the prospects enter a conference room in the hotel. This was our waiting room. Volunteers called the names of players that the scouts wanted to see. In all, 32 teams were represented, with more than 50 scouts. I sat in the room talking to other prospects and watched as names were called. Sometimes the person I was talking to would get called, causing me to spark a conversation with someone else. This continued to happen repeatedly. At first, I didn't notice it, but as hours and hours passed, I realized that I was one of the few prospects left in the room that hadn't been called. I tried to keep a positive look on my face, but inside I was torn apart. As we were closing in on the final minutes of the night, the volunteers came in one last time. I had a slight hope that I was finally about to get called by one of the scouts. "That's all for tonight, fellas," one of the volunteers said. "See y'all brought in early in the morning in the lobby to catch the bus to the stadium."

I grabbed my stuff, caught the elevator to my hotel room, walked inside the suite, and jumped on the bed, face down in the pillows. Drowning in my thoughts of negativity, I wondered why I even bothered to go after this dream.

As I lay in my hotel, in despair, I received a notification on my phone. It was from my sponsor dad, Geoff. The timing was crazy.

> *"Proud of you and everything you've accomplished. Teresa is looking down, smiling from above. Make her proud."*

Just a few days before I traveled down to Dallas for the Showcase, Amanda, my sponsor sister, called me to inform me that Ms. Teresa, my sponsor mom, had passed away from cancer. I hadn't even known she was sick. I had just seen her before I left to go home for Christmas break, and I had no idea what this selfless, kind woman was going through. My sponsor family was my home away from home during my time at the Naval Academy. I looked at each of them as an extended family. Ms. Teresa was like another mother to me. I couldn't have made it through the Academy without her. Whether it was bringing me soup and medicine when I was sick at school or just giving me a warm meal and a place to sleep on the weekend, Ms. Teresa made it her mission to ensure I felt comfortable away from my family. I'm forever indebted to her for the love that she showed me.

After seeing that text from Geoff, I went through my phone back to a text message I received from Ms. Teresa when I first declared for the draft before her passing: *"Guess I can say I knew you when. It could not happen to a more deserving person. You are truly blessed with family, friends, and an amazing support system. Love you."* I got up from my bed, wiping tears as I looked into the mirror and said, "Cameron, you are here for a reason. God brought you here for a reason. You can do all things through Him. You have a guardian angel watching over you. Do this for her tomorrow."

I conducted my nightly stretch routine, read my favorite scripture, Jeremiah 29:11, said my nightly prayers, then cut off the lights. I went to sleep that night at peace, knowing that I wasn't going out on that field the next day to represent myself. I would do it for Ms. Teresa. God reminded me that I wasn't alone, and I was representing something bigger than my own name.

I woke up feeling confident, free of worry and doubt. This confidence displayed itself on the field. The coaches took us through various NFL combine drills to see how we moved as a defensive back. I was fluid, explosive, and made some great catches. I looked like a natural. I looked like I belonged. More importantly, I know I made Ms. Teresa proud.

After the workouts, scouts poured onto the field to talk to some prospects. At this point, I wasn't even worried about them anymore. I felt like I already did what I had to and felt fulfilled in that alone. However, as I was taking my cleats off, I saw a scout walking in my direction. I looked around to see who he could be looking for and realized that no one else was in the area but me. The scout was coming to talk to me! The scout was from Kansas City, and after thanking me for my service, he asked a lot of questions about leadership. He followed up by saying he was impressed by the way I moved on the field and would be in touch in the future. The encounter with the Chiefs' scout gave me the boost I needed to keep my dream alive.

Following the College Gridiron Showcase, God showed His hand again. A representative from the Hula Bowl reached out to my agents, informing them that one of their defensive backs had to drop out due to injury, so they had one last spot available for me to participate. Regarding college all-star games, the premiere event was the Reese's Senior Bowl. After that, you had the NFLPA Bowl and the East-West Shrine Game. Due to Covid-19, the NFLPA and the Shrine Game were both canceled. Therefore, the Hula Bowl was now the year's number two college all-star game, attracting many of the country's top prospects. While I wasn't a top prospect on paper, God had His favor upon me. He placed my name in the room and allowed me to secure a last-minute invite. You can't tell me that my God isn't good.

When my agent told me the news, I told them I didn't want to go. During the Showcase, I tweaked my groin. I didn't want to go out there and compete if I wasn't 100%. In reality, I wasn't really worried about my groin. I was concerned about competing in general. Unlike the Showcase, the Hula Bowl would be a full-pad interview. My weakness during my football career had always been my ability to tackle. I refused to get in front of scouts live and have my fear put on blast. At least if the scouts see it on film, I don't have to be there with them to see their reaction.

I brought my concerns up with my parents. At first, I fed them the same thing I told my agents, "You know...I tweaked my groin. I don't think I should go out there if I'm unhealthy." My parents saw right through the lies.

"What is the real reason you don't want to go?" My mother asked.

I shook my head in disappointment, thinking I would get off this easy, and then I replied, "Well. I really don't want to get out there and embarrass myself. It's a bunch of the best prospects from Power 5 programs. I don't want to make a fool out of myself." My dad laughed at me. "You've been this way since you first started playing the game of football. Don't you think it's time to silence that voice in your head? You're thinking about the past mistakes you've made on the field and using that to determine your ability with this current opportunity. You have a clean slate and a chance to show the scouts in

Identity

person what you can do."

My mom was nodding her head the whole time my dad was speaking. When he concluded, she said, "You know what you need to do." At that moment, I remembered my dad's question from when I was five years old: "Who are you going to be?"

It is easy to forget what you've already been through as you face more difficulties. At that moment, I had to remind myself that God had already brought me this far, and He didn't bring me here just to leave me now. I reminded myself of my little wins and realized that while this might be a new giant, I had a choice to make that would ultimately shape my identity. Was I going to be a coward and hide behind an injury? Or was I going to walk through a door God opened for me and make the most of an opportunity? Besides, who in the world would pass up a free trip to Hawaii?!?

I called my agent and told him I was making the trip.

After the Hula Bowl, I saw myself trending in the right direction. There was still one problem that hadn't immensely affected me yet but was about to make its presence known: the Covid-19 pandemic. While some parts of the country were starting to loosen up, the Academy was still extremely restricted. Rightfully so, though. We all lived in the same dormitory, Bancroft Hall. We couldn't risk someone going out in town and contracting covid, bringing it back to the hall, and spreading it around rapidly. Therefore, nobody could leave campus, and nobody could come onto campus except essential personnel. Not only that but you were constricted to your room. The only times you could leave were to use the restroom, grab a meal, or enjoy your 1-hour period of outdoor exercise. And by outdoor exercise,

I mean outside. There were no weight rooms or indoor facilities open for athletes to use.

With no off-the-yard privileges and no weight room, I felt like I had run into a wall. How was I going to train for a pro day with no resources? Plus, finding ways to prepare wasn't the only problem. I still needed to set a pro-day date, but with the Covid-19 restrictions, there was no sign of the Academy being able to host a pro-day. I was praying for a miracle.

A teammate, Myles Fells, was also pursuing a shot at the next level. Myles had talked to me all season about playing in the NFL, and I shot it down every time he brought it up. When I called Myles over Christmas break to tell him my mind had changed, we became accountability partners. One of our strength coaches, Coach Brian Miller, sent us a workout plan via text. We would perform different speed workouts and record each other's reps. At the end of the workout, we sent our videos to Coach Miller, who would annotate different parts of the video and send us feedback for things to work on moving forward.

Most college athletes that pursue the NFL are off their college campus after they make this decision. They fly out to states like Florida, Texas, California, and Arizona to train with some of the best athletes in the best facilities. Their whole life is revolved around making their bodies as high-functioning as possible to produce the best results at their pro-day.

Meanwhile, I still had to finish my college degree at the Naval Academy. Luckily, I was only taking 16 credits at the time. I would go to school during the day, and once that final class finished in the afternoon, I would meet Myles on the field to get our workout in. This is in February in Maryland, so we had the honor of working

Identity

out in the gusting winds coming off the Chesapeake Bay. The cold weather built character. There were days when I didn't feel like going out there, but I still showed up. I'm thankful I had Myles push me through those low moments. Even though we were making the most of our training for the speed workouts, we still had to find a way to build our strength. There are only so many push-ups that you can do before you get tired of the exercise, and the pull-ups on my shower rack weren't cutting it anymore, either.

One day, one of my close friends, St. Helen, told me he might have a solution for me and Myles' strength issue. He mentioned that there was an equipment shed right outside of the track. I agreed to meet him there the next day. When we got into the shed, I saw a barbell and a couple of rubber plates we could use. However, there was no bench. This was when St. Helen pointed to a pile of padding, like the padding you see behind basketball goals in a gymnasium. We stacked the padding on top of each other as high as possible. Then, one person would get in the bench press position on the pads while another would lift the barbell and pass it to the person to begin their set. We only had 205 lbs. on the bar, but it's the best we could do.

Myles and I still didn't have a pro-day, and we were training on faith, hoping something would change at the last minute. As March and April got closer, we realized that we had to start looking for other options as there was no sign of the Naval Academy being able to host one. I discovered the NFL/NCAA has a rule saying if your school doesn't have a pro day, you can participate at another school as long as it's in your hometown or within a 30-mile radius. I called my high school defensive coordinator, Coach Chris Jordan, to see if he could reach out to the University of Memphis so that I could participate with them. Within a day, Coach Jordan got back to me, saying that Coach Silverfield, the Head Coach of Memphis, would allow me to come down and participate in their pro day. Even though I had no idea if the Academy would let me leave, I booked my flight to Memphis immediately. About two weeks before the Memphis pro day, I routed paperwork to the Commandant of Midshipmen to ask for special permission to attend. Six hours before my flight left, I got the approval to go and participate.

◆ ◆ ◆

I always hated flying in uniform or Navy apparel because it typically led to lengthy conversations about sea stories. As I sat at the flight gate in my Navy Football jogging suit, I was thankfully able to avoid these talks. Little did I know, the dreaded conversation was saved for the actual plane ride. I was sitting next to an older guy. He was a white male with a Santa Claus beard. He noticed my Navy hoodie.

"Do you have affiliation with the service?"
"Yes sir. I attend the Naval Academy."

"Naval Academy?!? I'm sitting next to a future admiral."
Laughing, I answered, "I'm just a midshipman, sir. I am still determining what my service career will look like."

"Well, what do you do at the academy?"

"I'm a political science major, and I play football."

"That's it? I'm sure you are involved in more."
"Well, I'm also the Senior Class President, sir." I almost felt he knew who I was.

"Class president!?! That's amazing! I'm sitting next to a future admiral and a future president! What brings you to travel today?"
"I'm headed back home to Memphis to participate in a pro day."
"Holy moly! We got a hall-of-fame NFL player, future admiral, and future President on this plane!"

As he got louder, people started to turn their heads and look towards the back of the aircraft to see who this man could be talking about. I was embarrassed. As we continued to chat back and forth, his volume declined, thankfully. He told me stories about his days as a Navy plane mechanic. He also gave me quality advice for when it was time for me to be an officer. When we landed, he asked a question that surprised me. "Do you mind if I pray for you?" I don't underestimate the power of prayer. At that moment, I felt that God placed me next to that man for a reason.

The pro-day wasn't the only reason I was looking forward to returning home–my older brother Jonathan was there. In Chapter 1, I told you about his success as a football player, but most people don't realize that participating in football is temporary. Sometimes it gets taken away from us earlier than we would like. If you aren't prepared for this, you can find yourself going down a frustrating path searching for your identity. This is what happened with Jonathan. When I was home for Christmas in 2017, our family had a little argument, and Jonathan walked out the door. Later, we discovered that he had walked to the bus stop and bought a ticket to California. I hadn't seen him since.

    I walked upstairs to find him sitting on the couch, watching T.V., with his air pods in his ears blasting music. When Jonathan saw me walk in, he stood and gave me a long, solid hug, no words, just holding me tight. Tears just began to fall, and, eventually, he released me, and I sat on the other couch in the room. He put his hand out when I started talking, signaling me to stay silent. I listened. I was happy to be in the same room with my big brother again. The guy that I looked up to my whole football career, whether he knew it or not. Jonathan never got a chance to see me play college football in person, but he never missed a televised game. He would always text or call me before the kickoff for some pre-game messages. Often, I would respond, "Bruh, I have to make a play this game. I need to do something big. I feel like my job is on the line." Jonathan always replied, "Let it happen." After a while, knowing I needed sleep, I got up to go to bed. He pulled out his headphones and said, "Let it happen."

    I had to trust in my preparation. In college football, getting caught up in the lights, cameras, and action is easy. Games feel like a reward for all the hard work endured during the off-season and the pre-game week of practice. Sometimes I thought that I had to do something different each game. "Let it happen" always reminded me that if I had prepared correctly, I would know when to seize my opportunity come game time. I didn't need to do anything special.

At the Memphis pro day, it was time for me to let it happen. The work that I put in over Christmas break, the feeling that I felt in that meeting room during the College Gridiron Showcase, the pain that I pushed myself through at the Hula Bowl, the outdoor sessions in the cold with my teammate Myles, lifting in the track-shed with my friend St. Helen, getting coached virtually through pictures and videos from Coach Miller, was all for this opportunity.

I walked out there with a confidence that could only come from God: Godfidence. In front of 32 NFL scouts, I let my name be known. I ran well, tested well, and went through defensive back drills like an NFL cornerback. Afterward, I was approached by ten different teams. I knew I had a shot.

Things continued to get brighter. The Naval Academy received an emergency distribution of the Covid-19 vaccine, which meant freedom for everybody on campus and a chance for normalcy. It also meant that the Naval Academy could host their own pro day. Now my friend Myles had the opportunity to showcase his hard work, and it was good to be on home turf with my brothers again. After competing at Memphis, I showed more confidence for one last evaluation and one last interview with the NFL scouts. The hay was in the barn.

6 | THE HARVEST

The 2021 NFL Draft was scheduled from April 30th to May 1st. The first round was on the 30th, the second and third rounds on the 31st, and the fourth-seventh rounds on May 1st. I wasn't concerned with the first two days of the draft as I wasn't a day one or day two guy. My name had yet to appear in mock drafts, and my agents told me that most teams had me with a 7th-round/undrafted free-agent draft grade. This didn't faze me. All I wanted was an opportunity.

The guys getting drafted in the first round already had their bags secured. In my mind, I was miles behind them. While they were at the draft or home celebrating with their families, I was working out the first night of the draft. The next day, my family and best friend, Tylon, flew into the area, and I spent the day with them and some of my other friends. This kept my mind at ease. The next morning, I opened my Bible to spend time with the Lord. When I went to sleep the night before, I had already chosen three scriptures I was going to turn to:

> *"For I know the plans I have for you,"* declares the LORD, *"plans to prosper you and not to harm you, plans to give you hope and a future."* Jeremiah 29:11 (NIV)

> *"Trust in the LORD with all your heart and lean not on your own understanding; in all your ways acknowledge Him, and He will make your paths straight."* Proverbs 3:5-6 (NIV)

> *"In their hearts humans plan their course, but the LORD establishes their steps."* Proverbs 16:9 (NIV)

The verse from *Jeremiah* had been my guiding light at the Naval Academy. It gave me peace and comfort, knowing that God's plan for my life was for my good. The two scriptures from *Proverbs* reminded me that it was His plan, though. While I planned to receive a phone call to play in the NFL, that doesn't mean God had that in store for me. I just trusted Him to make a way for me to achieve this dream, and even if it didn't come to fruition, I would continue to trust in God, knowing this wasn't His plan for me.

After devoting time to the Lord, I threw on a red and blue plaid button-down shirt, a pair of jeans, and the Top 3 Air Jordan 1s to match, nothing too fancy, just appropriate for the watch party I was hosting for my close friends and family for the final rounds of the draft at a restaurant in D.C. If I were to receive a phone call that day, I wanted to be surrounded by those who supported me throughout the journey.

At the beginning of the party, I was enjoying being with

my loved ones, especially my family. This was their first trip up to D.C. since my junior year. They couldn't make it to any of my senior year home games due to Covid-19, so I appreciated having time with them. I didn't begin to get nervous until the start of the final round. During this round, teams would contact players they wanted to sign, even if they didn't plan on drafting them with their last pick. I had no messages or calls from my agents indicating that any team had expressed interest in me. I was starting to believe my opportunity wouldn't come.

I watched name after name get called in that final round. While I didn't have draft expectations, I was still disappointed. Looking over at my little brother Richard really got me. I almost felt like I was letting him down. He had been a key piece of my motivation to even chase the NFL, and I just wanted to be an example for him. I felt the tears swell up, and I could feel my friends starting to look at me in concern. One of them even handed me a pair of sunglasses to cover my teary eyes.

The announcer on the screen came on to announce the final pick of the draft. Since I had been in contact with the Buccaneers, I had small hopes that this could be my moment.

"With the final pick of the 2021 NFL Draft, the Tampa Bay Buccaneers select: Grant Stuard, Linebacker, University of Houston."

Devastated.

The tears transitioned from swelling up my eyes to falling down my face. My cousin, Che, essentially an uncle to me, noticed the emotions overtaking me and quickly walked me outside the restaurant. He lived in D.C. and looked after me from the moment I arrived at the Naval Academy. He knew all I had been through and how badly I wanted this to happen. We started walking down the street, and as I cried my eyes out, he said words of encouragement, "Look, this isn't the end all be all. You've accomplished a lot in your life already and God has more in store for you. You know what we always say: 'Lord, let your will be done and help me understand.' Keep your head up. Wipe those tears off your face and go back inside that restaurant with your head held high and thank everybody for coming out to be with you."

As those last words came out of his mouth, my agent called. I wiped the tears from my eyes and answered the phone,

"Hey, Mike. What's going on?" I said.
"Cam! What's happening? How are you holding up?" He asked.

His excitement threw me off. I figured he was just trying to keep my spirits up so that I would remain hopeful.

"I can't lie. I'm a little disappointed. It hurts not to hear my name called after everything I went through."
"Well, I got some news for you. The Kansas City Chiefs want to sign you as an undrafted free agent."

"Wait, what?!? Let's go!! Let's go!! Tell them I'm coming." I couldn't contain my excitement. My yelling was heard from inside the restaurant, causing all my friends to run out to see what the hype was about. "We did it!" I exclaimed. "We're going to the Chiefs!" My agent called again after that, and I was a little worried.

"Hello?" I answered nervously.

"Cam what's good. I just got another call from the Tampa Bay Buccaneers. They want to offer you a contract as well."

"Word?! Yeah, let's go to Tampa. Tell them I'm coming. Let the Chiefs know that it has been a change of plans."

My dad played in college with the Tampa Bay linebackers coach. The same man also coached Jonathan when he played for the Arizona Cardinals. I felt more comfortable going somewhere with a known connection and knew I'd rather be in Florida than Missouri. There was also the fact that the Buccaneers had just won the super bowl with a roster full of future Hall of Famers. I was elated. Two teams that had just played in the Super Bowl called my agent to sign me as an undrafted free agent. I was beyond blessed. I couldn't thank God enough. The underdog and the guy they counted out was headed to the NFL. God doesn't call the qualified. He qualifies the called.

In 1 Samuel 16, God tells Samuel to go and anoint one of Jesse's sons as the next king after the rejection of Saul as king of Israel. When Samuel arrived, he saw Jesse's oldest son, Eliab, and thought he would surely be the Lord's anointed based on his physique. God told Samuel, *"Do not consider his appearance or his height, for I have rejected him. The Lord does not look at the things people look at. People look at the outward appearance, but the Lord looks at the heart."* (1 Samuel 16:7 NIV) Jesse had seven of his sons come before Samuel, but Samuel insisted that God had chosen none of them. Jesse said he had one son left, the youngest one, who was out tending the sheep. His name was David. Once David appeared, the Lord said, *"Rise and anoint him; this is the one."* (1 Samuel 16:12 NIV)

I imagine a scout speaking up in the Buccaneers or Chiefs draft room on my behalf and receiving some pushback from the other scouts. "Cameron Kinley? Who even is that? The same guy who lost his starting job as a Senior?" Maybe the scout responds, "Yes. He is the one." God's presence was in the draft room that day. He brought my name into the room.

The first thing I did after getting off the phone with my agent for the second time was embrace my mom.

"You did it! You did it!" she exclaimed with tears of joy pouring from her eyes.

To this, I responded, "No, mom. We did it. We did it. Thank you."

I went to my dad next, Coach Kinley, the man who introduced me to the game of football. He witnessed my growth firsthand from that practice when I wanted to quit all the way to now. "I'm proud of you, son," he told me as we embraced. That's all a son wants to hear. I just wanted to know that I made my father proud.

I hugged my friends next and popped a bottle of champagne. I was the man of the hour. I felt loved. I felt supported. I felt that everything had been worth it. The doubters, the humiliators, the ones who talked about me—none of them were in my mind anymore. For me, that moment was bigger than making it to the NFL. It was bigger than signing with the Tampa Bay Buccaneers. It was the result of placing faith over fear, hard work, and overcoming adversity. I didn't make excuses. I just controlled what I could control and made it happen. That's how I know it works. I'm a living testament of it.

◆ ◆ ◆

When I returned to school that Monday, I worked with the Naval Academy to ensure everything was set for my package to the Secretary of Defense for delaying my commission. At the time, President Trump's policy to allow service academy athletes to delay their commissioning to pursue professional opportunities was still in effect. This policy required your Academy to submit a package to the Secretary of Defense for approval, passing through the Superintendent of the Academy, Assistant Secretary of the Navy, and Secretary of the Navy, before ultimately reaching the Secretary of Defense. If approved, you would graduate, enter the Individual Ready Reserves, and play your professional career. Once your career finished, you would commission and serve five years as an officer. So, your service commitment was kept. This avenue allowed service academy athletes to become a part of the less than 2% of collegiate athletes that play professional sports while still fulfilling the responsibility of service afterward. However, anyone in your chain of command had the right to deny the request. While the package was supposed to be sent 90 days prior to graduation, the Academy wanted to wait and see if I would get signed before sending it off. This rubbed me the wrong way. However, I was ensured that this wouldn't impact the higher-ups' decision process. They told me that everything would be fine.

I spent that week studying for my final exams and working out to get ready for rookie mini-camp. I had

Identity

about ten days before I was set to report in Tampa, and I needed to be clicking on all cylinders. Rookie mini-camp was a vital part of the process of earning a roster spot on the defending roster. I was an undrafted free agent, and I knew I had a mountain to climb to make the team.

I could feel the nerves building up inside as the camp got nearer. Even though the Tampa Bay Buccaneers organization believed in me, I still couldn't say I fully believed in myself. There was still a lack of confidence inside me, a piece of me feeling like I didn't belong. I found myself looking up the other players that I was competing with and comparing myself to them. I read up on early projections for the Tampa Bay Buccaneers roster and fed my mind with all the reasons I would not make the team.

My doubtful feelings continued with me all the way to Tampa. I was excited to be there but didn't want it to be temporary. I wanted to make the team. The more I thought about the odds I was up against, the more nervous I got about the chances of making it a reality. When I landed in Tampa and got to the hotel with the other rookies, they appeared to be much more confident. Their confidence highlighted my insecurities even more.

I spent that night lying in the darkness of my hotel room with my eyes glued to the ceiling. "Just let it happen." I tried to remind myself.

"But I can't just let it happen." I thought. "I must make it happen. But what if I'm not good enough to make it happen?"

I couldn't get the negative voice out of my head. The voice telling me I wasn't good enough, attempting to hold me hostage to my past failures—the voice of my own insecurities.

Ding

I turned over to look at my phone on the nightstand. It was a text message from my little brother, Richard, containing a picture of what appeared to be an entry in his journal:

"Wednesday, January 27th: Cam is in Hawaii for an all-star game. God bless him with strength & courage. He is a great player; he just gets down on himself so quick. Please God, I know you will. He is the best and works too hard. League him!!"

Tears began to fall. It is one thing to pray for yourself, but there is power in prayer from others. Though Richard wrote this months earlier, he waited for this moment to share it, waiting for the moment I needed it most. Richard believed in me more than I believed in myself. It was time for me to show him that I believed also.

I woke up the following day and read my all-time favorite bible verse, Philippians 4:13.

"I can do all things through Him who gives me strength." (NIV)

After brushing my teeth, I looked at myself in the mirror and declared my daily affirmations: "I am qualified. I am capable. I am more than enough. I will be successful." I got dressed, put my Air Pods in, and turned on my favorite tape by my favorite artist, "Friday Night Lights – J Cole." I was a man on a mission and was on a business trip. When we arrived at the Buccaneers' facility, I hopped off the shuttle with a smile. It was game time.

Rookie mini-camp is extremely slow-paced. The practices consist of individual drills, a 7-on-7, and a short script of plays for offense vs. defense. The coaches really weren't expecting you to make plays. They just wanted to familiarize you with the playbook and NFL style of practice before the veterans showed up. I didn't really care what the coaches were expecting. I had high expectations for myself; I wanted to make a play and stand out.

My match-up for an offense/defense scrimmage was Jaelon Darden, a 4th-round draft pick out of North Texas. He was smaller, standing about 5'8 and weighing around 170 lbs. As a bigger cornerback, I always preferred matching up against bigger wide receivers. The smaller receivers were much quicker than I was, and I had trouble staying in front of them. It was just my luck that Jalon was one of the quickest and most explosive receivers I had ever attempted to guard. I had my hands full. For the first few reps, I tried to play off-man against him. This gave me a 7-yard cushion, so I didn't have to worry about getting beat deep. In reality, I was playing scared and being too cautious. I was getting beat on a lot of comeback routes, curl routes, and a couple of dig routes. He was cooking me and my confidence. On about the 12th play, I knew I needed to play press man and use my long arms and bigger frame to get my hands on him at the line of scrimmage so he couldn't execute his route freely. I lined up in front of him and shaded a little bit to the inside. When the ball snapped, I shot my inside hand up to jam his chest, but he faked outside, causing me to miss. He then swiped my inside hand down and beat me inside off the line of scrimmage. A general rule of thumb is that an inside release by a wide receiver means he wants to run an inside route. I noticed that most of their routes that day had been slants, posts, digs, or curls to the inside. Knowing this, I didn't panic when he beat me inside and just kept my outside leverage. I remained patient not to jump inside too early, and knew his breaking point was coming once I felt him slow down a little bit.

I jumped inside to jump the curl route and turned my head back toward the quarterback. My eyes widened as I saw the ball coming in my direction because I knew I was about to get the opportunity I had prayed for. I couldn't fumble it. Instead of making a pretty catch with my hands, I made a basket for the ball to fall into my stomach. The precautions served me well because I gained possession of the ball and ran it back the other way for a touchdown. "That's how you make a play, Navy!" the corners coach exclaimed. "Now keep building on it."

That was all I needed for my confidence to be activated in full effect. I knew that I belonged.

I continued through the rest of rookie mini-camp with a different type of swagger. I was making plays left and right, not only on defense, but also in the special teams' drills. I owed this to Navy. We took special teams seriously in college, so I just transferred the same habits, allowing me to stand out even more. Articles were getting posted on all over social media about the undrafted rookie from Navy who had a legitimate shot at making the team, which was definitely stroking my ego. I wasn't used to getting all this recognition. By the end of the rookie mini-camp, I knew I had accomplished my short-term goal. I made leaps toward making the 53-man roster. It was time to keep building on my momentum.

Once we started our rookie workouts, I realized that I was really living the dream. NFL facilities have everything you need, no questions asked. There's a cafeteria that serves you three meals a day for free, a nutrition/refueling station with custom-made protein shakes or smoothies, massages available, and a fully equipped training room. There was no excuse for not having your body in top shape.

The days consisted of breakfast in the morning, a workout after that, then position meetings and film following the workout. We would typically leave the facility around 2 p.m. with the rest of the day to ourselves. For the first time in my life, my only responsibility was football. At the Naval Academy, football was just another part of my schedule and never the main thing. I had to balance football with a rigorous academic schedule, military responsibilities, and extracurricular involvements. In Tampa, I felt all that weight lifted from my shoulders. I was getting the chance to fully immerse myself in the game I loved. In my eyes, the playing field was finally leveled.

The icing on the cake was when the rookies were called into the executive meeting room to sign our rookie contracts. Nothing felt better than inking my signature on that 3-year, $2.1 million contract. While it wasn't guaranteed, I still felt like a baller. Knowing I was months away from touching that amount of money was overwhelming.

Galatians 6:9 says, *"Let us not become weary in doing good, for at the proper time we will reap a harvest if we do not give up."* My parents taught me always to do the right thing. I strived to live my life in a way that honored them and, more importantly, honored God. Sometimes this made me feel like I was missing out on different things when I tried to "do the right thing." In Tampa, choosing the right was finally paying off. From riding the bench in 8th grade, being undersized and under-recruited in high school, playing scout team in college, and losing my starting job,

I felt like this was my harvest for sticking through all of that. I didn't have to see the light at the end of the tunnel anymore. I was living in the light.

After a week of rookie workouts, I returned to the Naval Academy to attend another milestone in my life: graduation. Graduating from a service academy is not a small feat. You go through four years of sacrifice and commitment for the day when you get to toss your midshipman cap in the air and replace it with your officer combination cap. While I wouldn't be participating in commissioning as an officer, the ceremony would still be huge for me. As the Class President, I would render a speech to my class at graduation in front of thousands, a speech I worked on for months and months. I also would have the opportunity to present our special guest, Vice President Kamala Harris, with a gift from our class.

I was on cloud 9. You honestly could not have painted a better picture. Little did I know, my life was about to get turned upside down.

7 | The Denial

When the news broke that despite the Covid-19 restrictions, our class would have an in-person graduation ceremony, I looked forward to traveling back to the Naval Academy. We would get to experience the anticipated celebration in Navy-Marine Corps Stadium, and it was deserving to go out on a high note.

Commissioning week at the Academy is full of tradition. There are garden parties at the Superintendent's house, a military parade, a Blue Angels flight show, military balls, and a lot of socialization in downtown Annapolis; positive vibes all around. After spending the first day with some friends, I went to bed early for a good night's sleep before graduation rehearsal in the morning. While lying in bed at my sponsor's house, I felt my phone vibrate. It was an email notification from the Commandant of Midshipmen, and initially, I thought it was a mass email.

It was a Google Calendar invite to meet with the

Commandant at the Academy tomorrow afternoon. Only four people were invited: one of my classmates attempting to play professional baseball, his battalion officer, my battalion officer, and me. I reached out to my battalion officer and asked what was up. Unfortunately, he was just as confused as I was. I felt uneasy, and the email threw me off completely. Why did the Commandant choose now to meet with the two athletes attempting to go professional?

We were called to a conference room on the top floor of Hopper Hall, one of the newer buildings on the Academy's campus. We traveled up the elevator, sat at the long table, and waited for the Commandant's arrival. Gazing out the window, we could see where spectators had gathered on the deck to watch the Blue Angels flight show. When the Commandant entered the room, he cut straight to the chase.

"I scheduled this meeting to inform you all that the Acting Secretary of the Navy has declined your request to delay your commissioning and play professional sports. Because of this, you are set to commission on Friday at graduation."

Silence.

Numb, I stared out the window at the smiling spectators on the deck. Seeing their joy reminded me of how I felt right before I boarded my plane to head back to the Academy to graduate. I was on top of the world; just like that, somebody was coming in to snatch my dream away from me. I brought myself to utter some words. "That's all he said?" I questioned.

The Commandant nodded his head. "Yes," he

responded, "That's all we received." I could tell he felt bad for us. I posed a second question. "He didn't give you any reasoning?" Shaking his head in disappointment, the Commandant reaffirmed, "Nothing."

It wasn't making sense. A monumental decision like this had to have some justification behind it. Refusing to settle, I asked one more question. "And there isn't an appeal process for this?" I could tell the Commandant was getting a little frustrated at this point. He kept his composure, though, as he knew I was going through many emotions. "No. You are set to commission on Friday with the rest of your classmates." After saying this, he stood up from the conference table and returned to watch the skilled pilots perform wonders in the air.

I had no conduct or honor offenses during my time at the Academy. I was an honor roll student. I was the class president, team captain, and held multiple other leadership roles during my time in school. I just didn't get it. I tried to do everything the right way, yet I still found myself in this situation. I had just spent a week and a half living out my childhood dream, and now, somebody who didn't even know me was taking that dream away. All I could think was, "Why me?". But as Mama always said, "Life's not fair."

I knew immediately that I was in a very sticky situation. In the military, we're taught to follow orders from superiors, but this wasn't one I was just willing to comply with. It wasn't supposed to end like this. I reached out to some players from the other academies who were in the same position as me. We created a group message after we all got offered NFL contracts. There were three Air Force Academy players and one from West Point. I sent texts to them, asking if they also got denied. Their response almost surprised me more than the Commandant's alarming news: "No, we didn't." Again. I thought, "Why me?".

I called my agents, Ryan and Mike, to let them know the deal, and at first, they thought I was pulling a prank on them. Ryan had also played football at the Naval Academy, which was a significant factor in signing with their agency, Divine Sports Entertainment. I knew Ryan and Mike would do everything possible to get me back on the field. In the meantime, they told me to stay positive and focus on enjoying graduation. The next call I made was to my parents. Just like Ryan and Mike, they thought I was messing with them, but my mother could hear the tone of my voice and knew this was a very serious situation.

Some people suggested I should be a delayed graduate and not commission or graduate on Friday. I knew I couldn't do that. While the dream of being in the NFL was very important to me, graduating from the Naval Academy held much more weight. Just because adversity arose in one part of my life didn't mean I had to let it contaminate everything. Besides, I was also set to give a speech at the commissioning ceremony, and I couldn't pass up on that; commissioning week wasn't about me.

As I kept the news to myself, my classmates were unaware of what took place. They were offering their enthusiastic congratulations, asking what the next couple of my months would look like. I had to pretend and go along as if I were heading back to Tampa.

I continued through the week, masking my emotions, knowing that the NFL situation was out of my hands. ESPN and the NFL Network were still interviewing me about my role in the graduation event, my speech, and my presentation to Vice President Harris. Smiling as if everything was OK, I felt like a fraud. I tried to enjoy graduation, but sadly, the moment didn't feel as sweet anymore. That night, I found myself feeling empty. No matter how hard I tried to hype it up, I felt like commissioning was closing the door on a room I had just started entering, a room I deserved.

I had no problem serving in the military. I came to the Academy intending to serve, and I didn't even plan to play professional football. However, once the opportunity of playing in the NFL presented itself, I wanted to chase after that childhood dream.

I awoke the following day feeling sorry for myself. With no desire to attend graduation, I certainly didn't want to get up there and give the graduation speech. That's when I heard a voice in my head: "Who are you going to be?"

Delivering the graduation speech took courage and discipline. Nobody in that stadium besides my family and close friends, knew what I felt inside. It was a moment I will never forget; I spoke with a different kind of confidence and strength. I had the honor to present our class gift to Kamala Harris, the first African American and woman elected Vice President of the United States. It was a once in a lifetime moment.

After the ceremony ended, I stood on stage with the Vice President, knowing she didn't know what I was going through. I took a risk and told her that I would need her help with a situation. She nodded her head and kept smiling. "Maybe I should've clarified that a little more," I thought.

◆ ◆ ◆

The next day, I boarded a flight back to Tampa to collect some of my personal items, noting how different things were from my first trip there. I still hadn't released anything publicly, so I grabbed my things and boarded another flight to Memphis as soon as possible. Back home, I continued to work out while we were reaching out to my state senator, congress members, and military officials, attempting to find answers through all the proper routes. I had already missed two weeks of Organized Team Activities (OTAs) in Tampa.

The report date for mandatory mini-camp finally arrived, and things still hadn't turned around. With my inbox filled with questions from reporters, my agent and I felt it would be best to put out a statement. Here were my words:

> *Recently, I was informed that my request to delay my service to play in the NFL was denied by the Secretary of the Navy. I have spent the past week processing my emotions, as it is very difficult to have been this close to achieving a childhood dream and having it taken away from me. In 2019, President Trump endorsed a policy titled the "Directive-type Memorandum (DTM)-19-011 – Military Service Academy Graduates Seeking to Participate in Professional Sports". This policy allows academy graduates to delay their commissioning to pursue professional athletic opportunities. 2019 was the first year for the policy to be put into action with players such as Malcolm Perry (Navy/Dolphins) and Elijah Riley (Army/Eagles) reaping the benefits.*
>
> *Currently, I have four other counterparts who have not been denied the opportunity to participate in the NFL: Jon Rhattigan (West Point/Seahawks), Nolan*

> *Laufenberg (Air Force/Broncos), George Silvanic (Air Force/Rams), and Parker Ferguson (Air Force/Jets). While I acknowledge that these men are from different branches of the armed services, it puzzles me as to why I am the only person to be denied this opportunity.*
>
> *I am very aware of the commitment that I made to service when I first arrived at the United States Naval Academy. I look forward to my career as a naval officer in the information warfare community. However, I am deserving of the opportunity to live out another one of my life-long dreams before fulfilling my service requirement.*
>
> *During my four years at the Academy, I tried my best to do all things the right way. I ensured that I was involved in all aspects of the Academy's mission: morally, mentally, and physically. Over the past few months, I have brought positive publicity to the Naval Academy and the U.S. Navy through many interviews and news articles, which I hoped would show the value that the armed forces could gain from allowing this opportunity to be pursued.*
>
> *In the meantime, I am unable to continue working out with the Tampa Bay Buccaneers. I have hopes that this situation will soon be overturned and that I can get back to competing on the field. Please direct all media requests to my agent, Michael De Sane, or President of Operations, Ryan Williams-Jenkins.*

I thought I was just letting everyone know what was going on and didn't realize that I was about to embark on a rollercoaster. My phone started ringing immediately after I posted. My direct messages were flooded with requests for interviews from various news outlets. The first day was spent with news interviews in the city of Memphis. I was driving from station to station, fielding phone calls.

In the first interviews, I could feel the love from all of those around me, and even in the community, people stopped me in public and said they were praying for me. After a few days, I began interviewing on major networks such as CNN, Good Morning America, Fox News, and TMZ. I watched a surprising video of an Armed Forces Committee on Capitol Hill where a congressman from Georgia asked the Acting Secretary of the Navy about my case. My story was a topic of discussion for many popular podcasts and talk shows. In a matter of days, I had become a national news story.

It was exhausting. Not only did I not like spending all day in front of a Zoom camera, but my story kept getting misinterpreted. Without reading my statement, the media painted me as an entitled kid who wanted to get out of his military contract. I was told I was wasting taxpayers' dollars, and that I took an academy spot from someone more deserving. Up until this point, I considered myself mentally tough. I was weathering the storm and leaning on God to carry me through, but I had become a target unwittingly. If I made any wrong statements, I knew I would eliminate any chance of getting the situation turned around. I was tired of taking the higher road. I felt palatable again, just like in elementary school when I transferred to a private school.

After another day of interviews, I sat at the kitchen table with my mother. Seeing the weariness on my face, she said, "Baby, there's something I've always wanted to share with you. I've been waiting for the right moment. I feel like that time is now. Adversity is nothing new for you. You've always been a fighter. Even before you came into this

Identity

world, you had a purpose. God placed you here for a reason.

"When we discovered I was pregnant with you, your father and I had hit a rough patch in our relationship. We loved one another but were unsure of what the future held for us. I already had Nia and Jonathan, so I did not want to be a single mother of three kids. We came to the difficult decision to terminate the pregnancy. We arrived at the clinic and completed the appropriate paperwork. I went through all the preliminary steps. The last step of the process was a video detailing what was to come. As I watched, I knew I couldn't go through with it. It just didn't feel right. I went to the waiting room where your father was. He looked at me and could see it in my eyes. 'Let's go,' he said as he grabbed my hand." During difficulty, they almost lost sight of the promises they made to one another, and the blessings God had given them. I was born their third child on the third day of the third month.

At that moment, I was reminded that everything I was going through was bigger than me. God was placing me through this situation for a reason. When I declared for the NFL draft, I remember feeling like God had something to show me, even if it wasn't the NFL becoming a reality. Maybe this was it? Maybe it wasn't about me. Maybe He wanted to test my faith in Him in the midst of a media uproar. Did I have contingent faith, or did my faith persist regardless of the outcome? This platform was an opportunity to praise Him even more when everybody else around me expected me to be upset and angry. I could use my situation to shine a light on Him. Like James 1:2 says, *"Consider it pure joy, my brothers and sisters, when you face trials of many kinds...."*

After a couple of weeks in the national spotlight, things

finally started to die down. Despite gaining some attention, I felt we didn't make enough progress toward getting me back to Tampa, so I started focusing on returning to Annapolis to fulfill my military duties. One night, I was hanging out with my friends, and one of them blurted out, "Yo, Cameron. Have you seen Twitter?" I checked my phone and saw that I had a notification from Senator Marco Rubio. He tweeted one of the ESPN articles about my story and stated that he would be writing a letter to President Joe Biden to get this situation fixed. It was a spark, but I didn't want to get my hopes up too much. Besides, the President had other things to worry about.

 A few days before heading back to Annapolis, I got a call from the assistant to the Assistant Secretary of the Navy. He said their office wanted to meet with me once I returned to the Naval Academy on Monday. "Not another one of these," I thought.

8 | The Reversal

The meeting was set to take place in Hopper Hall, and with the memory of the last time I was there, I was anxious, expecting the final declaration that made playing in the NFL impossible.

When I walked into the conference room, the energy seemed different. I was greeted by the Assistant Secretary of the Navy and her staff. The Assistant Secretary got straight to it, "Hey, Cameron. Thank you for making the time to meet with us today. We scheduled this meeting because we might have found a loophole for your situation." Seeing my excitement, she informed me this wasn't a guarantee. It would just be a way to get my packet re-reviewed by the chain of command for a possible reversal. The appeal process consisted of a request to have my commissioning revoked by the Board for Corrections of Naval Records to go back to the status of being a midshipman. If the board approved, my packet would then be resubmitted up the chain of command for reconsideration from the Secretary of Defense. If he approved, I would delay my commissioning and participate with the Tampa Bay Buccaneers again, fulfilling my service commitment afterward. If the packet got denied, I would recommission again and continue my path as an officer in the Navy.

"Are there any repercussions to submitting this package?" I asked the Assistant Secretary. I was assured that everything would be fine.

I filled out the necessary paperwork and handed it off to the staff. They told me they'd be in touch over the next couple of days with the final decision. While there was a chance, I didn't forget the Assistant Secretary's words, "Don't get your hopes up."

I didn't release anything about the meeting publicly. I informed my agency and my family/close friends that there might be a possibility for things to get turned around soon. In the meantime, I was still a commissioned officer, which meant I had responsibilities. My first day of work was Plebe Summer induction day. It was funny being on the other side of I-Day. I thought about how just four years ago, that was me coming through Alumni Hall with an alarmed face wondering what in the world I had gotten myself into. I was excited for these new plebes. They had no idea how much growth they were about to experience from learning how to get comfortable being in uncomfortable situations–a lesson that I was currently living.

I continued throughout the week, helping around the campus with various tasks. I did maintenance workouts to keep my body in decent shape in case things turned around. This was different from the approach I had when

I was going after my NFL dreams the first time. My faith was stronger then, even though my chances were slimmer. After the media fiasco, my faith was honestly drained. Deep down, I didn't believe things would turn around, and honestly, I was starting to get content with it. If I didn't return to Tampa, I wouldn't have to worry about getting cut. Everybody's last impression would be the undrafted rookie from Navy having a great rookie mini-camp and not being able to continue due to external factors. This would take the responsibility off my shoulders, and I could live the rest of my life saying, "Yeah, I would've made the team. I was balling out before the Navy incident happened." It was cowardly, and thankfully, God had a different plan for me.

◆ ◆ ◆

I woke up the morning of July 6th to a phone call from the Assistant Secretary's office, saying, "Be on standby today for a call from the Secretary of Defense regarding his decision on your package."

He hung up right after that. His tone was straightforward; I couldn't sense any excitement, but I didn't sense any disappointment. Suddenly, my faith felt rejuvenated. I felt like I was on the edge of a breakthrough. I tweeted "God's Plan" with the praying hands emoji, symbolizing that I was putting it in God's hands. It was out of my control at this point. I turned my ringer up and locked my phone.

About 20 minutes later, my tweet was quoted by a reporter from the Pentagon. The tweet read:

> *"Defense secretary to allow Navy C.B. and Naval Academy class president Cameron Kinley opportunity to sign with Tampa Bay Buccaneers and attend training camp. Official announcement coming soon from Pentagon."*

I thought, "Who even is this??" My phone started to blow up immediately with text messages. "Is this true?!?", "Congratulations!!", "Let's go!!" I didn't respond to any of them. I was just sitting there, not knowing if this was real. I decided to stay off Twitter and wait until I received the phone call I was on standby for. I called my family and agency to update them on the latest news. We all agreed that it'd be best for me to draft a statement for release if things got turned around.

After drafting the statement, I went to the driving range with some of my teammates from college to get my mind away from it all. Golf was always therapy for me. Afterward, we went to get some food, and then while I was heading back home, I got an incoming call from a 703-area code. Arlington, VA.

"Hello?" I answered.

"Yes, is this Cameron?" the unknown person asked.

"Yes, it is," I responded anxiously.

"Hey, Cameron. This is Secretary Lloyd Austin. How are you doing?" the voice replied.

There are some things people can't prepare you for. While I knew I was on standby for a call from the Secretary of Defense, receiving the call was crazy to me! I immediately snapped back into my military etiquette. "Hey, sir! My apologies. I didn't know this was you calling. I'm doing well, sir. How are you?"

"I'm doing well, thank you for asking," he responded, chuckling. He could tell that I was a little startled. "Hey, I am calling to inform you that today we have cleared the path for you to play in the National Football League. We think this will be great for our armed forces, particularly the United States Navy. You set the example at the United States Naval Academy, and I trust that you will continue to set the example in the NFL and represent our armed forces well."

Stunned. I thanked him repeatedly and promised not to let them regret this decision. We continued to talk for around 30 minutes about everything that had transpired and how they would work to ensure nobody had to go through this in the future. I thanked him again and the phone call concluded. After the phone call, I released the official statement:

> *Today I was informed the Secretary of Defense will be allowing me to continue my journey with the Tampa Bay Buccaneers and attend training camp at the end of this month. I am extremely appreciative of Secretary Austin's decision, and I am excited to represent our fine military in the National Football League. This past month has been very challenging, and I am thankful for everyone who has supported me in any way.*
>
> *Sometimes in life God tells us to be still. We do not always understand what He is trying to show us, but He always has an ultimate plan. The most valuable lesson I've learned throughout this whole process is to trust His timing and remain confident in the fact that God will*

always prevail. Thank you to my village for standing beside me. Without my family and close friends, there is no way I would be where I am today.

I would like to give a special thanks to my agency, Divine Sports & Entertainment, for their tireless efforts to work through this situation. Not only have they done a great job representing me, but Michael De Sane and Ryan Williams-Jenkins made sure to check on me and ensure that I was keeping my head up.

I would also like to say thank you to DeMaurice Smith, Joe Briggs and the NFLPA, the NFL League Office, Senator Marco Rubio, Representative John Garamendi, Representative Austin Scott, Omega Psi Phi Fraternity, Inc., various USNA alumni, and the many others for their efforts. Also, I'd like to extend my gratitude to all the media outlets who reached out to help share my story.

Lastly, thank you to the Tampa Bay Buccaneers organization for believing in me and remaining patient with me throughout this process. I am excited to get back to work in Tampa Bay with my teammates.

My phone carried messages overflowing with love. I was beyond thankful. I made sure to call every person I knew who played a direct role in getting things turned around and did my best to respond to everyone's text messages.

The power of God is real. Adversity has its way of appearing in our lives at the worst times possible. In these moments, you must tell yourself that we serve a God greater than anything we're against. *"Greater is He that is in you."* Even though my faith was weak, God was strong. Even though I had no hope, God remained right there. He didn't turn away from me and turned the situation around

Identity

for my good. I immediately went to the gym. While working out, I got a call from the 703-area code again.

"Hey Cameron, how are you doing? This is General Mark. Milley, the Chairman of the Joint Chiefs of Staff."

"Hey, sir. What's going on! Thanks for calling," I replied.

"I just wanted to call you personally to extend my congratulations. I am so excited for you and believe this is a great opportunity for all the service academy grads. President Biden approached me regarding the situation and asked what I thought should happen. After our conversation, we worked with the office of the Secretary of the Navy to figure out the best solution to get your package approved by Secretary Austin. Thank you for remaining patient and letting this all work out."

Shortly after the call, I saw a tweet released by the White House:

> "Today, I was pleased to learn from Secretary of Defense Austin that he has granted Cameron Kinley's request to pursue a playing career in the National Football League prior to his service as a naval officer. I am confident that Cameron will represent the Navy well in the NFL, just as he did as a standout athlete and class president at the Naval Academy. After his NFL career is over, he will continue to make us proud as an officer in the United States Navy."

I was overwhelmed. The President of the United States was involved in my situation! My name was being

96

brought up in the White House! As the story started circulating and attracting more attention, I knew I couldn't fall into the same 5-6 interviews a day cycle I endured when the news broke about the denial. I needed time to work out and get my mind right to head back to Tampa. I settled on during three interviews: one local for Memphis, one with CNN, and one with ESPN. After that final interview, I locked in on the task at hand. It was time to make an NFL roster.

◆ ◆ ◆

Making the 53-man roster as an undrafted free agent would be an uphill battle after missing out on OTAs, mandatory mini-camp, and rookie workouts. I had to take each challenge one day at a time. The first was my weigh-in. The strength staff wanted me to come in weighing 203 lbs. with an acceptable range of 201-205 lbs. I had gotten up to 215 lbs. while everything was going on with my story, because I was too busy feeling sorry for myself and being mentally and emotionally drained. I hadn't been training like a professional football player, and I now found myself trying to scrap it together to find a way to lose 15 pounds in 10 days.

I practically starved myself before flying to Tampa. I only ate vegetables with a handful of sliced chicken breast. I did cardio twice a day on top of my football workouts. I was fighting for stamina and facing the consequences of the choices made during the media fiasco. I couldn't afford not to make weight, literally. The NFL can fine you for every pound over the designated weight. I couldn't afford a fine, but I also couldn't afford for them to think I was uncommitted.

My ten days ticked away like seconds, and before I knew it, I was on a flight back to Tampa. This time was much different from rookie mini-camp. In May, I was just an undrafted free agent that nobody expected much from. This time, I had an identity from my recent journey. People all around the country knew my name. After landing, I didn't eat anything as weigh-ins were the following day, and I wanted to avoid adding extra weight. In the mall nearby, I grabbed the leanest smoothie I could find and spent the rest of the night on the Peloton in the hotel's exercise room. I was the only one in there and just pedaled away, listening to my thoughts.

The past month and a half had been like no other, but no real surprise. From riding the bench in 8th grade to losing my starting job as the team captain, the journey had always been filled with adversity. I was always able to find a purpose through the storm; this was just one more opportunity to rise above.

9 | THE HARVEST PT. 2

I woke up early the next morning and thanked God for another day. After catching a ride to the facility, I immediately went to the weight room for weigh-ins. I walked up to the scale, stepped on it, and looked straight ahead. I could feel my heart jumping out of my chest as I had yet to see my weight drop below 207 lbs.

"Two-Zero-Six," declared the coach.
"You have to be kidding me," I thought. Disappointment rattled throughout my body.
"Try to go to the restroom. Maybe you can shake off an extra pound," suggested the coach.

After returning from the restroom, I stepped on the scale again. This time I looked down to see the number for myself. "Two-Zero-Five," declared the coach.
 I jumped off the scale because I wasn't going to give those numbers any time to fluctuate. The first target was

out of the way, and it was time for target number two: the conditioning test.

I knew I wasn't in the best shape of my life, but I also knew I didn't have time to make excuses. The coaches didn't tell us how many sprints we would run, just the time requirement and the line to run to. I made up my mind that I would finish in the front of the group every single rep. Taking one rep at a time, I'd be right back at the line, standing tall, waiting for the next one, whistle after whistle. I was exhausted. My stomach was cramping, and my legs were getting heavier by the minute. But all I kept telling myself was: "Next rep." I had to place mind over matter. Coach Mario used to always tell us, "Your mind will quit 1000 times before your body will." A few of the rookies started falling out to my left and right due to exhaustion or muscle cramps, but I wasn't one of them. I finished every single rep in the front, if not near the front, and walked away from that test with a boost of confidence. Target number two was knocked down, and day one was in the books.

The next few days were known as "QB school," consisting of light walk-throughs designed for the quarterbacks to get their arms loose and for the rookies to settle in before actual training camp began. These days were vital opportunities for me to refresh myself on the playbook and learn the new calls installed during my time away. It also gave me an opportunity to get acclimated to stardom.

I remember stretching and warming up the first day when suddenly, I heard a familiar voice, "Ready, set, GO!" It sounded like someone I had heard on tv before. I looked to my right and saw the owner of the cadence: Tom Brady. I instantly started smiling. I was starstruck. This was my first time seeing TB12 in person. "Mane, stop smiling!". One of my teammates had caught me. Slightly embarrassed, I regathered myself. "I can't help it, bro. That's the goat!". We laughed it off, and I locked back in to prepare for the day. While I was starstruck, I knew I wasn't down there to be a fan. I was down there to chase greatness as well, but sometimes to be great, you must study the GOAT.

Eventually, the rest of the vets reported to the facility. It was time for our first team meeting before practice was set to begin the following day. When Head Coach Bruce Arians got on stage, I made sure I had my notepad out to take notes. I was curious to see who else was doing the same thing. As expected, all the other rookies had notepads out taking notes, as well as a couple of 2nd/3rd-year guys who were on the fence of making the 53-man roster. But one more person had a notepad: the 22-year vet, 7-time super bowl champion, 5-time league MVP, and future hall-of-fame quarterback, Tom Brady. By the end of the meeting, I only had a few lines written down, and I glanced at Tom's notebook. He had a page full of notes! At that moment, I knew what separated him: he treated every year as if it were his first.

The night before my first official NFL practice was full of restlessness. It was different from the nerves I felt before rookie mini-camp. This time they derived from external pressures. With my story going nationwide, I knew people were following my status. Everybody would want updates about the Naval Academy grad chasing his dreams. I didn't want to disappoint.

My first day back on the field was a nightmare. I was playing like I had two left feet. The drill work wasn't coming naturally, and the pace of the game had my head swirling. It reminded me of my first days of practice at the Naval Academy after coming out of basic training. I didn't look like the same player who had been down there just two months before.

Every day, we had special team meetings right after lunch. I always sat in the front row with some fellow rookies to stay engaged. One day, I didn't see one of the guys I had gotten close to. Once we left the meeting, I noticed he texted the group chat stating he had been released. "Just like that," I thought; he was just at practice that morning, and now he was gone. I started to fear that I was up next. Every practice, I worried I'd get called into the GM's office to hear the unwanted news. This internal fear led to me playing with fear. Instead of focusing on thriving, my mind was fixated on surviving. You can't afford to play with fear in the NFL, something I discovered when I stepped up against Antonio Brown.

Most of the time, the veteran players liked to line up against the other vets. In this scenario, we were near the end of our 1-on-1 session, but AB wanted one more rep. When nobody hopped out to go against him, I saw this as my opportunity and lined up against the legend. My heart was pounding, "Just focus on your technique...Just focus on your technique," I repeated internally.

His release off the line wasn't crazy, and he wasn't running at a fast pace either. In my mind, a comeback route had to be coming. Unexpectedly, AB hit another gear, and his tactic to deceive me was executed perfectly. As I was straining to keep up, the ball sailed over my head and fell perfectly over his shoulder into his hands. The placement from Tom Brady allowed AB to stay in stride the whole time, and I watched as he danced toward the end zone. He looked back and grinned at me, "Not yet 26.

Keep working though, champ," he said.

Moments like this continued for the next few weeks, and I found myself worrying more than appreciating. I feared going to practice. During this round of camp, I decided to not be on social media. Nonetheless, I found myself searching my name on Twitter and Google to see what reporters were saying about me. Negative posts harmed my confidence more, and spending my time reading what reporters were saying took away from time that should have been spent listening to what God was saying. More than ever, I needed to be filled with scripture to get my spirit back on the right track. During most of the denial process, I remained steadfast in my faith. Even if I had my doubts, I stayed committed in the Word and was even doing 30 Second Thursday devotionals on Instagram to display my faith. This time, God was on the sideline, as I focused more on the public's approval than on God's. I needed to get my spirit right, or else I risked squandering a dream of a lifetime.

During my junior year at the Naval Academy, one of my mentees introduced me to his sponsor parents. In addition to my actual sponsor family, the Newtons became an adopted sponsor family for me. While I was in training camp, they coincidently were in Tampa for a business trip. They reached out to see if I had time to get together, as they brought a graduation gift. I met them in the lobby of my hotel one night after another rough day. They asked me how things were going, and I was honest.

"I'm struggling; I can't find the same confidence I had when I was down here the first time. I feel too many external pressures. All I can think about is possibly getting released from the team."

Identity

As a steadfast Christian, Mrs. Newton reminded me, "Remember that God has you down here for a reason. Don't forget where your power comes from, and don't forget whose you are. God didn't give you a spirit of fear." Mr. Newton then handed me my graduation gift: *The John Maxwell Leadership Bible*. Tears warmed my face. "You don't know how bad I needed this right now. I can't express how thankful I am." It's not that I didn't have access to a Bible, but I felt that God was giving me a sign through the Newtons. He reminded me that He was the source of my strength and didn't bring me this far to leave me. We continued to catch up for a few minutes and prayed together before we parted ways.

When I got back to my hotel room, I broke down crying. It was a mix of frustration and disappointment. I felt like I had wasted the first weeks of training camp. I was too concerned with what the media was saying and trying to play to perfection. I focused on what I was up against rather than my faith. I opened my new Bible and turned to the same verse that had guided me throughout my time at the Academy: Jeremiah 29:11. As I read the verse, I substituted my name as the subject of God's direction. "For I know the plans I have for *Cameron*," declares the Lord, "plans to prosper *Cameron* and not to harm *Cameron*, plans to give *Cameron* hope and a future." I just needed to stick to the script.

The next couple of days were different. I started playing more aggressively and started making more plays. I wasn't focused on pleasing coaches or the media but on glorifying God for the opportunity in front of me. I was getting pass break-up after pass break-up. I even made a play 1-on-1 against Mike Evans. My position coach even acknowledged my progress. Things weren't perfect, but I finally started to show glimmers of hope. After two weeks of getting back on track, the biggest evaluation was right in front of me: Game 1 of the preseason against the Cincinnati Bengals.

10 | THE INTERVIEW

Game days at the Naval Academy were tightly structured. Everything was scheduled down to the minute, so you knew exactly where you would be at every point of the day right up to kickoff. The NFL had no such requirements. Kickoff was set for 7:30 PM Eastern Time, and the only guidance we received was to be at the stadium by 5 PM. The rest of the day was ours.

I woke up and spent some time in the Word before grabbing breakfast. When I got back to my room, I went through the same foam roll and stretch routine I did every game day in college. Afterward, I watched some film and reviewed the playbook to ensure I had all my responsibilities down pat. When I finished, it was only 12 PM. I still had 5 hours to kill.

My parents and a couple of family friends had flown in to watch the game, so I stopped by the hotel to visit them. I was thankful to have everybody there, but having my parents at the game was especially nice. Due to Covid-19 restrictions, they could only travel to one game during my senior season at Navy. After spending a few hours with them, I headed back to my hotel room to take a nap before having pre-game meal. Shortly after the pre-game meal, I drove to the stadium and began the mental switch to get locked in for game time. Anxiety was fierce. I was about to have one of the biggest interviews of my life. The team would be required to trim their roster from 90 players to 85 after the game before heading into the next phase of training camp. If I didn't perform, I knew very well that I could be one of those 5 players.

In my mind, I wasn't going to see any playing time until the second half. I was deep on the depth chart at cornerback and on special teams. Knowing this, I placed my helmet on one of the trainer tables after warm-ups and stood on the sideline to watch the starters kick off the first action of the 2021 season. Tom Brady trotted on the field for his only series of the day. After coming up empty, our defensive starters took over. On the next drive, backup quarterback Blaine Gabbert led the offense 79 yards down the field to break the stalemate. After kicking the extra point, the kickoff team huddled up to prepare to take the field for the first time. I heard someone screaming my name, "Kinley! Kinley! We need you on the kickoff team."

I didn't have time to figure out why I was going in so early as I scrambled to find my helmet and ran out on the field. The whistle blew, the kicker booted the ball, and the next thing I knew, I was sprinting down the field for my first NFL minutes. As the play developed, I saw I had a clear lane to the returner. My eyes widened, realizing I had a chance to make a big play. As the distance closed between us, I started to overthink. I hesitated and took a bad angle, causing me to miss the tackle. "Don't get in your head Cam," I thought. "It's still a lot more football to be played."

I wasn't going to be caught unprepared again, so I kept my helmet on until I knew I'd be back on the field. Throughout the first half, I continued to see action on special teams. With every rep, I saw myself gradually improving and getting more comfortable. Midway through the third quarter, the time finally came for me to get into the defensive rotation.

The Cincinnati Bengals were driving into our territory. They had the ball on our 40-yard line and were looking to increase their lead. They came out in a trips left formation, leaving just one wide receiver on my side. Since we were in cover 3, I knew I could treat this single WR like a 1-on-1 situation. On the snap, he drove off the line until he reached 15 yards, where he then turned around for a stop route. As I broke towards him, I saw the QB making a throwing motion towards another wide receiver who was entering my zone. I redirected, and as soon as I turned my head, the Bengals WR was about to make the catch right in front of me. I lowered my shoulder and delivered a massive blow. I heard the crowd go "oooooh" and hopped up, excited that I had made a play. The excitement was short-lived as I saw a yellow flag fly right in front of my face. My first play in the game on defense, and I got a penalty for unnecessary roughness. While the flag was disappointing, I knew I had overcome a key mental hurdle: my first tackle.

After my first series, I settled in. I was being aggressive and making tackles I never had the confidence to make my whole career. For the first time in a while, I could feel myself having fun and enjoying the game, free of stress and worry. I wasn't concerned with the media, and I wasn't concerned with pleasing the coaches. I was on the field glorifying God with the gifts He blessed me with to play the game of football at this level. I felt like somebody who belonged.

I jogged off the field that night in high spirits. As I entered the tunnel, filled with gratitude, I looked up to the heavens and pointed to the sky. "Thank you," I said. I finished the game with 6 tackles—the 2nd most of anyone on the team. After showering and getting dressed, I just sat in my locker and held my game jersey. This was a moment I knew I would never forget and one I wished would last forever as part of my legacy.

◆ ◆ ◆

Most people would wake up excited after playing in their first NFL preseason game, but something didn't feel right for me. Nonetheless, I knew I couldn't lay in bed and soak in those thoughts forever. I had to get up and get dressed for brunch with my family. When I arrived at the restaurant, I was greeted by my support crew. I hadn't spoken with Coach Darwin and his wife after the game, and they were still filled with excitement. I knew it had to be crazy to see a kid you coached in youth football playing on an NFL field. "Mane. Mane, you don't even know how proud I am of you, dude. Seeing you out there brought tears to my eyes. You looked like you belonged, dude. You are about to have a special career." This kind of talk continued throughout the brunch. We chatted about some of my tackles and what it felt like to be out there on an NFL field. While everybody was smiling and happy, I still felt uneasy.

After brunch, we said our goodbyes to the Henderson family, and my parents loaded into the truck for a ride to the airport. En route, we reflected a little more on my football journey and the most recent adversity I had to overcome to experience that moment. We discussed plans for their return next weekend for our second preseason game against the Tennessee Titans. Once we arrived at the airport, I hugged them goodbye and helped them get their bags out of the truck. "See y'all next weekend. Let me know when y'all land. I love y'all."

I got back in my truck and headed toward the team hotel to get some much-needed rest. About 10 minutes into the drive, I saw a call notification on my CarPlay display: "Tampa Bay Football Operations." "That's interesting," I thought. Sunday was an off day.

"Hello?" I answered.

"Hey, what's going on, Cameron. What are you up to?" asked the Bucs representative.

"Nothing much. I just dropped my parents off at the airport. Now I'm headed back to the team hotel to chill out a little bit," I responded.

"Unfortunately, there's no need for you to head to the team hotel," the representative replied. "We need you to come to the facility with your playbook. We've decided to release you today. You'll no longer be a Tampa Bay Buccaneer."

I could feel my body going numb with the shock. "Hello? You there, Cameron?" asked the representative. "Yeah, I got you. I'll be there soon."

Ashamed, I immediately called my parents to let them know the news. They were so excited when I dropped them off. My mom thought I was joking, but I told her I would never joke about this.

"Where are you going now?" she asked.

"I have to go to the facility to turn everything in. After that, I'm going to get my stuff from the hotel and drive back to Memphis today. I don't want to be in Tampa anymore."

"Come get me and your father after you go to the facility. We're canceling our flight. We will ride back with you."

I told myself that I wouldn't let them see me cry in that facility. I would walk through there with my head high and chest out. I wanted to show my appreciation for the organization because they allowed me to come back down even after I was initially denied my waiver. I was grateful for the Tampa Bay Buccaneers organization's patience with my situation. That didn't make it any easier, though. First, I had to turn in my tablet (playbook). Following that, I went into the training room to sign medical forms verifying that I was leaving the team healthy. When I left the training room, they handed me a black trash bag and sent me to the rookie locker room to collect my belongings.

The rookie locker room was in the indoor facility, across the practice fields from the main facility–about a 7-8 minute walk. When I got to my locker, I could feel the tears swelling. Nobody else was in that indoor practice facility but me. I stared at my Buccaneers helmet, my NFL practice jersey, my cleats, and other Buccaneer gear. I sat on my stool and just stared into the locker. Less than 24 hours ago, I was living out my childhood dream. Now, I was facing a cold reality of the business of the NFL. If the organization didn't believe in you, then it didn't matter how much you believed in yourself. I knew that if I had just a little more time, my growth would be substantial. They saw the progress that I made in the last few weeks. I felt cheated. I let the bitterness get the best of me as I threw my cleats and gloves into that trash bag. The Buccaneers could keep the hoodies, the sweats, the shirts...everything. As I walked away, without looking back, the tears began to get heavier.

After leaving my locker, I walked into the general manager's office. "Cameron, I just want to thank you for everything you did for our organization. You have an extremely bright future ahead of you, and I'm not just talking football. One day, I'll be able to tell my grandkids I had the opportunity to meet you. Thank you for your service, and best wishes for your future." I thanked him for the opportunity and wished him luck on the upcoming season, then walked out the door and headed for the parking lot. In my truck, I called my parents to let them know I was on the way and turned on my gospel playlist to soothe my mind. I wanted to get myself together before I picked up my parents. As I was driving on the highway, the negative thoughts in my head were overpowering the gospel music coming out of my speakers. The tears in the well of my eyes were getting heavier.

One of the songs was "Stand" by Donnie Mcclurkin. The song says, "What do you do when you've done all you can and it seems like it's never enough..." That's how I felt. I went out on a limb to chase this dream and put everything I had into it. Once I finally made the dream a reality, I had to deal with more adversity out of my control. After making it through that, I felt that, surely, I was on the edge of my breakthrough. I felt I was fortified. I felt that I did everything I could. But it still wasn't enough. The tears were too heavy. My eyes turned into a waterfall, filled with regret.

I brought my emotions back under control until my parents got into the car. Driving away from baggage claim, the tears started again. I started to bang on the steering wheel, yelling, "What's the point? What's the point of taking the higher road, doing things the right way, trusting in God, going through adversity, if it's all just going to end up with me feeling like this?" I was frustrated with everybody. I was frustrated with the Navy because I truly felt that if I had gone to OTAs, Mini-Camp, and had rookie summer workouts, I'd still be playing in the NFL today. Something that should've been a no-brainer. Yet, I had to go through the difficult path. I had to be the one player out of the 5 service academy guys to get the difficult road to end up being the first to get cut. I could feel my blood boiling. I wanted to scream. I wanted to go into a dark place and be by myself. I felt this way the whole ride from Tampa, Florida, to Memphis, Tennessee.

11 | THE REVELATION

The trip home took 12 hours.
For the most part, I kept the fact that I got cut to myself. I knew that the media would handle letting the world know. Every network that interviewed me earlier in the summer would let everyone know how the story ended. I could see the comments now: "All that for nothing," "I told y'all he wasn't going to make it," "He should've just shut up and served." In my mind, they were right. The breaking news regarding my release didn't garner the same love that my other news stories had attracted. When I got signed by the Buccaneers, I heard from people I hadn't talked to in years. Even after being denied a waiver, everybody checked in on me and prayed for me. When I got cut, the number of messages reduced drastically. Totally ashamed and embarrassed; I felt like a failure. My identity had been in the game of football, and without the game, I felt like I didn't bring any value to anyone around me. I assumed people saw me differently

now that I wasn't in the NFL anymore. I didn't want to talk to anybody or be seen publicly.

My dad wouldn't let me hide my face for long. He dragged me to the football practices at Lausanne. In the past, going to Lausanne always brought back the best memories from my high school glory days. But now, as I walked across the turf, I couldn't feel my connection to the game that once brought me life. My love for the game seemed to be fading away. I honestly just felt drained.

When I wasn't at Lausanne, I spent my time at my grandparent's house. My grandad and I would play chess while some old-school soul music played in the background. This was my escape. While I was there, my issues seemed to disappear. I didn't have to address the pain of getting cut or even deal with the pressures of what was next.

One day, I was sitting at my grandparent's house when a mentor of mine, Dr. Tarol, reached out to see if I would come to speak to her students in her local organization, Project STAND, a juvenile justice program that provides mentorship to provide equity, education, and empowerment to young African American men and reduce recidivism in the process. I had spoken to Project STAND multiple times via Zoom while in college, and Dr. Tarol felt my recent story would be good for her young men to hear. I didn't see any value in it, but I agreed to the engagement.

The group was located at a school in one of the rougher areas in Memphis. As I drove to the school, I could feel butterflies in my stomach, like the ones I used to get in the locker room before football games. I wasn't scared, but I felt anxious. I loved to speak. Ever since overcoming my speech impediment in elementary school, I considered my speaking abilities a gift from God. At this point, I had done national interviews and even gave a speech in front of thousands and the Vice President of the United States. I was nervous then, but it didn't feel like this.

I was greeted by a room full of young African American men. I had prepared a whole dialogue for the students to focus on making good choices, surrounding themselves with the right people, and the importance of positive self-talk. Looking into their eyes, I could tell they were at a place of hunger. They desired something new in their lives. I felt the urge to go in a different direction. I started off with a simple question to break the ice: "How many people in here want to be rich?" As expected, everybody's hands shot in the air one by one. I then put a picture on the screen of me signing my NFL contract for the Tampa Bay Buccaneers.

"In this picture, I'm signing a $2.1 million contract to play football in the NFL for the Tampa Bay Buccaneers. Let me be real with y'all for a second. When I was down there in Tampa, I dreaded going to practice. I lived in a world of fear and couldn't feel any happiness. There's nothing wrong with wanting money in life, but you can't put paper over purpose. If the inner work isn't right, you'll miss out on an opportunity to seize everything you ever wanted."

The words just began to flow out of my mouth, and my prepared speech seemed immaterial. I found myself disregarding the script and going from the heart. I broke down pieces of my story from high school all the way to where I was today, stating the various lessons I learned, things that I did wrong, things that I did right...all of it. I closed by telling the story of discovering the news that I had been released by the Buccaneers and described my shame and embarrassment. Standing in front of the classroom, I realized that if things had never happened the way they did, I wouldn't have had this opportunity to pour into these young men. It was then that it hit me: maybe it's the journey that teaches you a lot about the destination. I said, "It's not always about the result, but who you become and how you choose to relate to the process. In focusing on results, we miss out on the beauty of the process. It wasn't the number of NFL games I could have played or the stats I could have compiled that ultimately mattered. That didn't determine who I was. The true value is in who I become after withstanding adversity and overcoming obstacles. Sometimes we go through trials and tribulations in life to learn a lesson that can be used to help someone else achieve their dream. And honestly, if it weren't for my struggles, I wouldn't be standing before you today."

It's not about what's happening to you; it's about what's happening for you. Take ownership of the adversity you experience in your life. Better yet, as James said in James 1:12, consider yourself blessed to go through trials of many kinds. When I got cut, I was soo focused on the result that I started to neglect the growth that I made during the journey. I defined myself by the failure. However, there is power in removing yourself from your struggles. My perception changed when I looked at my adversity as a tool for helping the young men at Project STAND. Instead of seeing failure and disappointment, I saw value.

After speaking with Project Stand, I went back and spoke at Lausanne. I spoke to high school football and basketball teams. I started posting motivational content on social media. Suddenly, the feelings I had when hiding from the world were beginning to fade. My pain was starting to turn into a new purpose. My transparency about my struggles was a source of inspiration for the people around me.

My agents were still in talks with NFL teams, but most were saying that they wanted to see how their team looked after the first few weeks of the season before deciding to bring anyone else in. I knew I could wait, but also knew I had a commitment to fulfill.

I reflected on what I asked God for in the game of football. Initially, I just wanted to get a full ride to college. He gave me that opportunity. Everything that happened in my career after I wore the Navy jersey for the first time was a bonus. I didn't have to have a good college career. I certainly didn't have to play in an NFL preseason game. Less than 1% of football players get the chance to experience that. There was no reason to have regrets. I was blessed. I was allowed to walk away from the game whole and healthy. God saw me struggling and turning away from Him, so He had to take the game away from me before the game took me away from Him.

I decided to recommission and officially begin my career as an intelligence officer in the U.S. Navy. It was time to direct my efforts away from the football field and into the military and society. Before reporting to Virginia for required schooling, I reported to the Naval Academy for a temporary duty assignment. The transition back into the military wasn't easy. For the first time in my life, I didn't have a commitment to the game of football, and there was a void that desperately needed filling. As much as I wanted to convince myself otherwise, I still felt bitter about how everything played out with the NFL, and the energy I got from those speeches in Memphis was starting to run out. I needed a reminder that everything happened for a reason, or else I would spiral down a dark path.

After successfully completing my required schooling, I got stationed in Whidbey Island, WA. The last thing I wanted to do was move across the country to a place where I barely knew anyone. I was nervous going to my first command, as I didn't know how people would view everything that I went through the previous summer. Maybe they had the same mindset as some people on social media who were against me playing football? However, I was welcomed with open arms. If anything, people appreciated the fact that I got the chance to experience the NFL. It didn't matter if I played anymore; they knew all the difficulties and circumstances I had been through and respected that I stood tall through it all.

Once settled in Washington, I immediately reached out to the local high school football coach in Oak Harbor, Coach Marcus Hughes, to see if I could come and speak to the team. To my surprise, Coach Hughes emailed me back and said I could coach if I wanted to. I honestly didn't believe I was ready to engulf myself in the game of football again, but I knew I needed to get involved with something in the community. As I worked with the players, my love for the game started to reignite. The lessons from my football playing days contributed directly to their growth as players. Watching them take what we did in practice and apply it immediately in the game was inspiring. They absorbed everything I was telling them, unconcerned that I wasn't playing in the NFL anymore. They respected me because of who I was. The more I coached, the more God reminded me that the value wasn't in a position, it was in a purpose.

Looking back on these last few years, I am thankful

everything happened the way it did. I don't define myself by my accomplishments, the opinions of others, or even my failures. When I think of my guiding question, "Who are you going to be?" I answer in a way that nobody can take away. As a man of God, I strive daily to carry out the purpose He has placed within me. A purpose that no position can take away. My identity is in Him.

Gratitude

"12 Not that I have already obtained all this, or have already arrived at my goal, but I press on to take hold of that for which Christ Jesus took hold of me. 13 Brothers and sisters, I do not consider myself yet to have taken hold of it. But one thing I do: Forgetting what is behind and straining toward what is ahead, 14 I press on toward the goal to win the prize for which God has called me heavenward in Christ Jesus." Philippians 3:12-14 (NIV)

Just like Paul, I know my race is far from over. I am not anywhere near the prize, but I continue to press forward toward the future. Maybe the future entails another run in the NFL? A 20-year naval career? Head football coach? President of the United States? Mayor of Memphis? Who knows. The bottom line is God's not finished with me yet. He's not finished with you, either. There is a lot more growth to take place, a lot more failure to experience, and a lot more success to achieve.

I want to thank you for walking along this journey with me. After reading this book, I hope you appreciate some of my struggles as much as the success I've been fortunate to achieve. More importantly, I hope this book inspired you to dig into your life. Are you currently in a transition phase? Are you in search of purpose? It may be time to go back and look at the journey you've been through rather than focusing on the destination you're arrived at. I'm confident that you'll discover your true identity and continue to pursue the purpose placed inside of you. Your story isn't finished. It's just beginning.

ABOUT THE AUTHOR

Cameron Kinley is a visionary, decorated athlete, motivational speaker, and above all, follower of Jesus Christ. After graduating from the United States Naval Academy with a B.S. in Political Science, Cameron had the opportunity to fulfill his childhood dream of playing in the NFL. Initially denied a delayed commission, Cameron received Presidential permission to sign as a free agent with the Tampa Bay Buccaneers. While Cameron was ultimately released, he turned this adversity into victory to continue on his life's mission of service, fueling his passion for empowering others. Today, Cameron continues to serve as an intelligence officer in the United States Navy and is an active mentor throughout his community.